Advance praise for
Real Estate Development Primer

A fantastic resource for anyone involved in development processes. A guide like this can make a huge difference in navigating the stages from concept to completion, ensuring that all necessary steps are thoroughly covered and helping to streamline the entire process.

—**Bob Scragg,** *President, City Centre Homes*

Brilliantly addresses the ever-growing complexity involved in developing real estate, and the undeniable requirement of soft skills and technical skills it takes to make things happen. If you are a seasoned industry veteran or newly aspiring to get involved in real estate development, this is an exceptional and highly relevant read.

—**Michael Nygren,** *President, District Group*

A succinct guide, emphasizing the integration of social, physical, and economic principles of real estate development. I am excited to test the practical application of this knowledge, alongside our traditional knowledge, as we embark on building trusted partnerships and expanding the economic opportunities of our Nation.

—**Charlotte Connor,** *Director, Development Strategy, Métis Nation of British Columbia*

Michael von Hausen presents a comprehensive guide to the real estate development process and how to take projects from ideas to implementation. Drawing from his decades of experience, he breaks down development to its key principles and techniques, with lessons and examples from his practice on how to make projects happen.

—**Andy Yan,** *FCIP, RPP, Director of the City Program, Simon Fraser University; Associate Professor in Professional Practice, Urban Studies Program*

Michael von Hausen's wise, experienced advice, laid out in the *Real Estate Development Primer*, is a must for wannabe developers. He has uncovered the secret sauce to augment fledgling developers' proposals, which will increase the odds of that development succeeding.

—**Mike Harcourt,** *OC, former premier of British Columbia and former mayor, City of Vancouver*

A highly readable and entertaining tour of key factors every real estate development team should consider, including both internal (your and your company's perspective) and external (city, community, site), delivered with von Hausen's trademark energy, insight, and enthusiasm.

—**Mark Holland,** *FCIP, RPP, Principal, Westplan Consulting Group; Professor, Vancouver Island University, Master of Community Planning Program*

REAL ESTATE DEVELOPMENT PRIMER

AN INTRODUCTION TO THE DEVELOPMENT PROCESS

MICHAEL A. VON HAUSEN

Real Estate Development Primer
An Introduction to the Development Process

Cover photos and concept images by the author
Cover photo of author by Mind's Eye Photography
Cover design by Betty Chiu and Tellwell
Interior graphics by Betty Chiu
Editing and proofreading by Naomi Pauls

Tellwell Talent
www.tellwell.ca

ISBN
978-1-77962-278-5 (Paperback)

For Laura, my life partner, my daughter Athena, and my grandson Jackson, who teach me and support me in ways I can't begin to thank them for.

CONTENTS

Introduction

This book introduces and breaks down the complex real estate development process. It conveys its many complexities in as straightforward a manner as possible. Texts on development often emphasize the technical and/or financial aspects. Property development is often treated as a transaction rather than a business process involving relationships. It is complex and not becoming any simpler.

Real Estate Development Primer presents the multiple dimensions of the process to budding students and experienced professionals alike. It strives to make better sense of the interrelated steps of the full development process. I wanted to create an inspirational book that is readable, concise, and readily digestible. For me, what is most important is to share knowledge I have gained about what really works and what doesn't work in our current disruptive world that appears to be constantly changing at lightning speed.

The book is divided into three sections, on development vision, site development, and optimum results. Starting at the beginning of the development process, I define its uniqueness and larger context. I move on to describe how developers generate the "idea" as a basis for projects. From there the text examines various steps in the process, providing insights into topics such as marketing and finance along the way. Finally, I discuss approvals and construction. Throughout, I explore specific subjects including quantitative and qualitative analysis, refinement, and shaping different scenarios for review. In the mix are self-reflexive topics such as developing your career, finding your niche within the industry, and ultimately giving back by creating great communities.

Each chapter's format is consciously organized with an overarching principle at the beginning. At the end you'll find a series of recommended techniques to elevate your development practice and key take-aways, to ensure you learn the basic rules well and comprehend the main messages of each chapter. I have deliberately made this book succinct to present the core components and qualities of development so you can grasp the whole process and profession more quickly and then dig deeper into separate areas of interest. A glossary at the end of the book defines key terms, and simple illustrations throughout complement the text.

I hope you keep this book handy for easy reference and inspiration. It may give you some ideas to help you understand and navigate the multiplex profession of real estate development, further transform your practice, or help you choose another area within it. Good fortune in your continuing search and understanding.

Michael von Hausen
January 2025

Nine principles of real estate development

1. Find a role that fits your skills and feeds your soul.
2. Break the mould without compromising positive results.
3. Find the spirit of place to achieve success.
4. Think market focus, return on investment, and financial analysis from the start.
5. Let the site speak to you.
6. You cannot go it alone.
7. Obtain a commitment or exit the approvals process.
8. Follow your design with the right trusted team.
9. Focus on your strengths and give back.

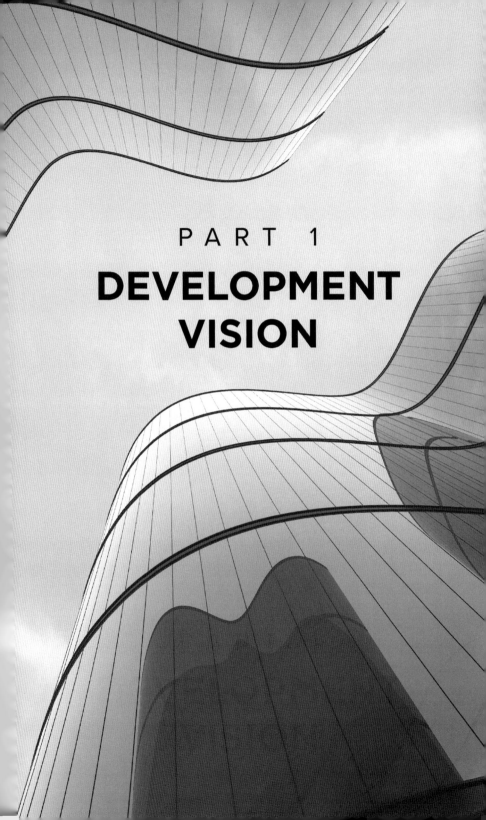

PART 1
DEVELOPMENT VISION

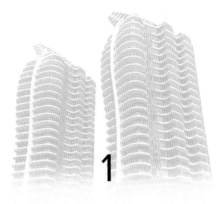

Overview of the Development Process

Principle 1. Find a role that fits your skills and feeds your soul.

> *Amidst a world of uncertainty, there is a collective hope that resides. It's an evolutionary part of the human spirit: to endure, to defy the odds, to rise.*
> —Tony Robbins

This chapter provides an overview of real estate development—what it is, how it is changing, and information about the development process itself. It discusses in broad strokes what developers do, how they do it, and the nine steps and three main qualities of the development process that determine success. The chapter also explores where you fit into real estate development and the privilege of creating what is envisioned as the next generation of great communities.

What developers do

Before we get into the process and analytics of real estate development, we need to set the context. Let's answer the following questions:

- Who is a real estate developer and how are they evolving with the times?
- What are their personality traits?
- What are their goals in business, both the older and the new generation?

First, it is key to distinguish the developer from the realtor. The developer "develops" and may sell a property, while a realtor simply sells property, for the most part. In certain situations, realtors can buy (assemble) properties for developers. In some cases, a developer obtains the approvals to develop land that may have been assembled by the realtor or his company and subdivides the property into individual parcels. They then sell the lots to builders, who might construct homes, commercial offices or retail, industrial buildings, or buildings for institutional uses (e.g., schools) or municipal uses (e.g., fire halls).

Real estate developers (hereafter also referred to as "developers") conceive the original ideas and then build the "dreams" that are on paper (if they have a construction operation within their company). Normally, they coordinate all the consultants, contractors, and sales. The sales can involve sales of lots to builders and/or sales to the final purchaser of the house or apartment unit. In other cases, developers sell or lease commercial, industrial, or employment space. Developers can also build and hold the property, therefore gaining long-term revenue in terms of leases or rents, and appreciation of the property value over time.

One of the problems developers face is that they have little control of the approvals process, especially if they are rezoning the property to another use. The control of the approvals process in British Columbia rests with municipalities or regional districts, in liaison with agencies within the provincial and federal governments.

Development learning and training

Usually, individuals join a development company first to learn the skills of development, including property acquisition, marketing, development planning/design, and construction. Various universities offer real estate development curriculums. For instance, the University of British Columbia (UBC) offers a Diploma in Urban Land Economics (DULE) and a Bachelor of Business in Real Estate (BBRE) degree, both online, part-time, and as an extension of the Sauder School of Business. Mid-career or early career training is also offered by UBC and other organizations such as the Urban Development Institute (UDI) in Vancouver, through its FortisBC School of Development.

The negative real estate business cycles

Entering the development profession can be a challenge. In a climate with volatile mortgage interest rates and inflation, the real estate market can be uncertain—and flat or sluggish in many sectors. Consumers are stressed given these economic uncertainties, especially with inflation affecting disposable income. With Canada's ongoing housing supply challenges and increased immigration adding to economic uncertainty, many potential real estate purchasers are sitting on the sidelines, waiting to see what happens before they move forward.

In British Columbia, emerging government policies, although well intended—such as the vacant house tax, Airbnb exclusion, the recently instated "flipping tax," and limited rental increases—arguably continue to jeopardize and put pressure on an already unaffordable rental market. As well, rising municipal *development cost charges (DCCs), community amenity contributions (CACs)*, and the recently instituted *amenity cost charges (ACCs)* only increase development costs in a high-priced market. New provincial legislation that aims to increase outright density and decreasing public engagement requirements could release some of the strain, but municipalities lack the necessary supporting social and physical infrastructure in many cases. How do we plan ahead in these uncertain times? One way is to project the future development cycle, as the next story reveals.

A few years ago, I was having dinner with a titan in the development industry. I was fascinated by his insights into the business and his approach as a leader in the field. He pointed out a new seven-year business cycle in real estate as a way of planning strategies moving forward. That means that we had just observed a seven-year "up cycle" (normally five years) and that we could expect an equal seven-year "down cycle" or more before the market would swing upward again in a significant manner.

The current real estate market is challenging, but there has been an incredible wave of prosperity for many years, with few disruptions like the 2009 downturn. World instability adds to the current stresses. But where there is uncertainty, there are opportunities. The year 2025 and beyond appear to be showing some promise again as interest rates come down, inflation declines, and the housing supply improves.

Where do you fit?

Sitting on the sidelines of life will not change the world or your individual future. Are you driven? Do you enjoy challenges and complex situations? Can you manage stress and adapt to dramatic changes? Do you want to give back and pay it forward? If these qualities are yours, you are well suited to a career or further advancement in real estate development. But do you still want to become a developer in the face of all the instability factors just outlined? Note that even in a stormy landscape, great developers with capital and resources find opportunities where many do not.

Do you fit the profile? Are you good with handling risk and changing conditions? Most often a potential developer profile includes acuity with numbers, some municipal planning and development experience, a marketing sense, and good communication and/or social skills. Of course, what skills you need depends on the sector in which you want to specialize: acquisition, planning/ design, development approvals, marketing, construction, or finance. Each of these sectors requires technical skills, knowledge, and abilities. Plus, determination, negotiation skills, and persistence are helpful traits regardless of sector, especially in a challenging market.

Learning from experience

Myself, I entered the development profession fresh out of graduate school. I was all of twenty-five years old and didn't really know a thing about development, except having read real estate case studies and completed theoretical financial analysis. One of the best-selling books at the time was *Men of Property: The Canadian Developers Who Are Buying America*.[1] The author, Susan Goldenberg, used maxims like "Leverage is the name of the game" and "Never use your own money." That was 1981. How things changed.

The prime bank rate rose to 21.75% in August 1981 and crushed all those developers that were highly leveraged using other people's money. Many companies were land-rich but cash-poor, like the company I worked for. Nu-West Development Corporation, the largest home builder in Western Canada, was part of that story. The surviving corporations—like Cadillac Fairview, Trammell Crow, Cabot, Cabot & Forbes, and many others—learned their lessons about how negative leverage (declining market and prices) can have the opposite effect on profits.

Others did not learn from these valuable lessons and leveraged again, like the famous Olympia & York company in the 1980s. Following its collapse in 1993, the Reichmann brothers began to rebuild their empire. Olympia & York Properties Corporation (O&Y Properties) and O&Y Real Estate Investment Trust REIT (O&Y REIT) returned to the real estate market in Canada, owning 18 properties in six Canadian cities. In 2005, the family sold these two real estate arms to Brookfield Properties for $2.1 billion, in what was called "the largest real estate auction in Canadian history."[2] They sold at the right time.

I have these experiences to reflect on any time I look at a potential real estate investment. I recently developed a twelve-page due diligence checklist that tends to curb my initial appetite for "shiny" real estate deals that appear promising at face value but whose gloss tends to dim with further due diligence.[3] Alas, if you don't learn from experience, you tend to repeat your mistakes.

I had to remind myself of this due diligence requirement just the other day when a promising real estate deal landed on my desk. There was pressure from the real estate sales representative, since the price was rising almost daily. On additional examination and after discussions with my accountant, the deal did not make sense tax-wise. Its attractiveness was further tarnished by a potential decline in market demand, an associated lower purchase price, and the five-year-long development horizon. In the end, late-breaking news of the imminent 20% "flipping tax" on properties not retained for two years absolutely killed the deal. The recent increase in the federal capital gains tax from 50 to 67% confirmed that I'd been right to withdraw.

Fresh thinking with a conservative foundation

There continue to be brash risk-takers in the world of property development. Everyone shines in an upward-trending market, but it is the challenging market that determines the real professional. These professionals and companies can be aggressive when the deal is right but are conservative at heart. They have clear goals, they have cash reserves, and they spread their precious capital over several projects. They might have been burned before but have learned from the experience. They also have specialties, whether it be concrete high-rise residential development, the focus for Bosa Properties, or multiple-family residential, in the case of Polygon Homes. These developers continue to grow, adapt, and innovate, with quality project delivery top of mind.

The real estate development process

Let's assume we have established the fact that we might fit the real estate development profile. We want to become a developer. How do we now build a new community or develop a building? We want to sell our units at a fair and profitable price. If the process goes smoothly, we will finish the project within or close to the estimated budget, within the scheduled time frame or close to it.

The development process itself is a key to the end results. As a developer, it is imperative that you know the process well, so you can adjust your project and still make the project economically viable and receive support from the community. The normal process can be described, simply, as property acquisition, planning/design, financing, project approvals, and construction—an elementary and straightforward, linear characterization. But on further examination, the process is less linear and more iterative, with interrelated steps. The next section briefly examines each item in an enhanced, nine-step version of the process. But first, I outline three essential *qualities* of the process.

Three key qualities of the development process

Before we delve deeper into the steps that constitute real estate development, here are three qualities of the development process that are worth remembering. I call them the ABCs of qualitative real estate development: agility, connections, and commitment.

- **Agility.** This quality gives a real estate company the ability to move and alter its direction or position for more positive results. Agility gives the developer the flexibility it needs to modify its strategy in response to a changing market. The ability to adjust and move to new market segments, adjusting design to changing consumer needs, is essential.

- **Connections.** Also critical to success are the connections a developer has already established in the local municipal, community, and political environment. Without connections and current local intelligence, a developer may find the approvals process a confusing labyrinth full of uncertainties. Trusted and established connections make the pathway to approvals much easier.

- **Commitment.** When times become uncertain or misfortune strikes, a company's true commitment and full resources will be called upon. That commitment is important to continued success and integrity. At the same time, as we will discuss further, developers must consider an exit or backup strategy from the outset, to prepare for unforeseen consequences.

Constant review and refinement

Constant review and refinement hone the project plan as well as site planning and keep them on track. Reflecting back and projecting forward are both part of this integrated and dynamic process approach. Otherwise, the process can stagnate, and team members can start pointing fingers at underlying factors they apparently could not control or people who did not do their job. Plus, failing to deal with or downplaying issues that arise can create disasters. To avoid such undesirable results, as developers we need to be pre-emptive in our approach to problem-solving and anticipate challenges before they happen.

Let's dig deeper now into the steps of the development process and, as a prelude to the rest of the book, describe a refined and robust process that is iterative in nature, with overlapping sequences.

Nine process steps

These nine steps in the development process give it breadth and depth, remembering that you need to act on rather than react to challenges. In simple terms, you want to be prepared for changes and modifications rather than reacting negatively to any alterations. The process described here is both technical and built on relationships. All these steps will be presented in more detail and supported by case studies later in the book.

1. **Idea.** Original or not original, the idea will drive the development and create the basis for the vision, goals, principles, targets, and strategies that frame the project. It can be as simple as a cluster housing development nestled along the waterfront or as complex as a multi-phased progressive seniors care facility reusing existing heritage buildings. The original idea will evolve and be refined throughout the development process.

2. **Site.** Understanding the site and its characteristics is essential to site planning, design, and economic viability. Too many projects are sunk

by unforeseen consequences of non-rigorous analysis. I advocate a place-driven approach to find the magic of the site within its context. This will help to shape a unique site signature that is exciting and creates community improvements through physical connections, environmental sensitivity, social support, and economic benefits.

3. **Review.** Bring out the sharp pencils and measure the site carefully to ensure that the capacity for development is there and the proposed development program can fit on the site. Be thorough and meticulous at this stage. To be otherwise will unduly compromise the project and erode the return on investment.

4. **Refine.** Consider the choices and scenarios that could be the project's future. Provide development choices—optimistic, pessimistic, and realistic—in a series of cash-flow analyses. These should be driven by a sensitivity analysis (including revenue, cost, and financing variables) to compare scenarios both desirable and un-desirable. Conform to conventional wisdom or the status quo and then refine the plan to define the best way forward.

5. **Partner.** Now introduce the best scenario (development story) to your bankers and investors. These should be regarded as your partners as you move forward, and they can help refine and position your project for success. Other partners, such as property owners or development niche experts, can also be considered to add muscle to the team or reduce

equity (cash) requirements. The property owners can provide the land as part of their contribution to development, with lease/rent revenue sharing as the project is developed and held as a rental property and/or sales revenue sharing if the project is sold.

6. **Test.** Back at the drawing board, refine marketing communications and test your strategies with an eagle-eye construction representative at the table. Use current costs, materials, and a pragmatic construction approach at a more detailed level to ensure the construction works and the market is present for the product. Then further refine the project to meet or exceed market expectations and construction requirements.

7. **Elevate.** This step is about not being satisfied with the same old product, although alignment with market requirements is critical to a certain extent to capture market demand. Some selective experiments with emerging market niches (based on market indicators) may be worth pursuing, with the ability to expand if successful. For example, lock-off units in larger apartments give the option to consolidate or expand space based on evolving family expansion or contraction and/ or add extra income as a mortgage helper.

8. **Approve.** The formal development approvals processes are becoming more complicated and incomprehensible in some instances. Municipalities are constantly trying to simplify their processes but often revert back to the status quo, although the terminology and

organization may appear different. These efforts and good intentions often end up layering more regulations on regulations, to further slow down an already protracted process. Connections and agility (see above) are catalysts in the approvals process, since altering development plans may create a faster process. However, the process of alteration or finding the third alternative can also be endless, depending on staff, community, and political support.

9. **Execute.** Execution is about finally constructing the dream and executing well. The construction review process should start early so that team members can incorporate requirements into the concept, schematic design, design development, and final construction drawings submission as part of building permit requirements. Paying attention to detail and implementing required change orders in construction are prerequisites to leaving a positive legacy on the site and helping to form a great community that adds to the existing community. This is what I refer to as a *net community gain* and *net environmental gain*.

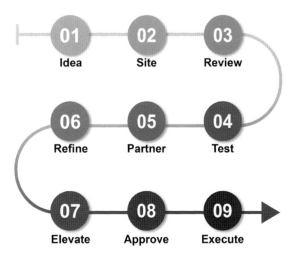

Figure 1. This diagram illustrates multiple steps of the development process, beyond the simplified description of property acquisition, planning/design, finance, approvals, and construction.

Techniques to elevate your practice

- Complete a self-assessment of your developer profile.

- Pick your target area or position in real estate development.

- Be determined and show your commitment.

- Know the real estate development process.

- Understand that agility, connections, and commitment are integral to the process.

- Remember to complete your property due diligence, develop a plan and convincing story, build trust, and sell the project with integrity.

Key take-aways

Learn from the trusted and experienced developers. Become interdisciplinary and learn to speak the languages of many professionals, like architects, engineers, landscape architects, planners, contractors, and bankers. This is the skill set of the professional real estate developer who stays in the game and prospers. They become a seasoned pro and maintain their entrepreneurial character.

We often don't visualize the real estate development process as an overlapping and interconnected relationship diagram. Yet the interrelated sequence of steps and their continued refinement are of utmost importance, especially as a common understanding of the development team and its various disciplines. This process vision keeps teams on track and refining within the framework. Customize your own process with your team based on project needs.

Now let's find out how understanding the current and future economy as well as next-generation thinking will shape real estate development into the future. We need to know these influential factors, otherwise we could have good intentions that do not match the changing demands in the marketplace.

2

Influences and Future Thinking

Principle 2. Break the mould without compromising positive results.

> *If the decade between the Great Recession and the pandemic seemed to be all about "superstar" tech cities, many of the winners in the remote-work era are going to be places that make tangible things.*
> —Bruce Katz

The times are changing radically fast as the types of buildings, land uses, densities, and tenant requirement demands continue to alter development plans. Developers must be comfortable on a roller coaster that has steep turns and white-knuckle descents. The first chapter introduced you to development and the overall process, from the idea to construction. This chapter looks at the external factors, local details, and next-generation thinking that can help inform and shape successful projects of the future.

Big-picture and small-picture learning

The context for the development business is changing across North America. The economy of the United States continues its influence, since our country trades most of its goods with the U.S. Hence the big picture informs the small picture. The U.S. has approximately ten times Canada's population, so the international market influences are huge compared to Canada. At an international level, geopolitical instability in the Middle East and Ukraine add uncertainty and inflationary pressure on commodity prices.

We need to know this changing context to be successful developers and know when to "go." In short, we need to view opportunities through a macro-economic lens. These macro influences affect national and local interest rates, inflation, and the consumer's ability or desire to purchase. Simply put, when buyers are not buying, development projects do not sell. What influences these buyers? There is an affordability problem or, better said, "an ability-to-buy problem," which is further illustrated in the following profile of Canadian buyers.

Most Canadians now have more debt than savings. Recent data from Statistics Canada outlined the growing impact of the cost-of-living crisis and the widening inequality gap in the country. The wealthiest 20% of Canadians, with an average net worth of $3.3 million, accounted for over 67% of total net worth in Canada, while the least wealthy 40% of Canadians made up just 2.8% of net worth, with an average of $67,738. Canadians also have the highest debt ratio of Group of Seven (G7) countries, with the poorest Canadians $2.84 in debt for every $1 of disposable income.[4]

How do we get versed in macro- and micro-economics? And how will this debt crisis affect Canadians' ability to buy or rent real estate? This debt situation is not a healthy situation, as inflation and interest rates further erode individual and family earnings and savings. On a three-month annualized basis, core inflation fell to an average rate of 2.0% in the third quarter of 2024, significantly down from the June 2022 high of 8.1%, and within the target range of 2.0 to 3.0%. According to MLA Canada, "One of the key contributors to CPI [the Consumer Price Index] is now shelter costs (mortgage interest cost and rents)."[5] Many Canadians are in a financial crisis right now, with the confluence of factors such as low affordability, higher inflation and interest rates (noting both inflation and interest rates have come down), and high rates of immigration. These forces influence *supply and demand*, further decreasing affordability. It is a complicated situation, as we will discuss.

The provincial governments of British Columbia (in 2023) and Ontario (in 2022) tried to increase housing supply by creating new policies and approval frameworks that are normally under the jurisdiction of municipalities. Some municipalities and regional districts objected to the "overreach" of the province into local government affairs and some, like the Township of Langley, put a pause on development until they could adjust their policies and approval frameworks to address the new reset. How do developers keep up with all these complicated changes and understand the language that seems to transform, like social media, almost daily? I have an idea, but it takes discipline and commitment.

In graduate school at Harvard, I told myself that I had to learn the language of business, so I had the *Wall Street Journal* delivered to my door every day. Reading at least the first-page briefs did help to make me more conversant in business language and tactics. I also took courses in capital markets, development economics, and the economics of urban infrastructure. I then began to speak the language and incorporate business strategies into my development plans. Most of my architect classmates referred to me as "the developer," since I focused in that area and became a teaching assistant in the real estate development curriculum. This position made me more intensely committed to not only learning the craft but also leading discussions. Comprehending the world of business is like learning a language; you must practise every day.

Every time you start a new development project, you are essentially starting a new business. From the idea to construction, the project is independent and demands business comprehension and relationship attention for success. From a pure business language perspective, components of the process include legal structure, product definition, planning and design, market development, project accounting and monitoring, sales, product construction, and customer care.

Take an interest in bigger-picture business economics and context forces, which help shape the smaller picture of real estate development. Right now, some developers have paused their property acquisitions because of uncertainty in the marketplace, while others are aggressively acquiring emerging "stressed" properties, especially outside the major metropolitan areas. Opportunity is where you find it, so define it in your own terms, with a sensitivity to community context and formative policy as well as economics.

Figure 2. Big-picture economics can affect the viability
of your smaller site.

Discipline your learning and focus on the industry.
Use LinkedIn and other social media platforms to get
connected. Join the Urban Development Institute or other
networks to meet people in the industry, and register
for UDI's FortisBC School of Development courses to
further network and learn from some of the best and most
progressive developers. As one senior project manager
told me the other day, he had coffee with the president of
the company he wanted to work with several times, and
presto! he is in the job he wants.

When someone says no, that's when you'll need sales
techniques to move them to yes. For example, if an owner
of a property says they are not interested in selling, you
have to first understand their motivations to say no. You
then have to offer those components that they are most
interested in, which might include a higher price, living on
the property for a specified time while approvals continue,
a share in the profits, or special natural or built features
that are to be retained and conserved. Satisfy the buyer's

needs and an abrupt no can transform to an enthusiastic yes. William Ury, in his book *Getting Past No*, explains his concept of advanced negotiation to enable cooperation. His further writings in *The Power of a Positive No* turn the tables further from a negative no to a "positive no" (an opportunity to reconsider, with the door still open) or an affirmative reply.[6]

"Schooling" is fundamentally different than "learning" in that the first teaches you to follow orders and is rote instruction. Learning, in comparison, is the ability to think critically and independently.[7] Produce what we want you to produce, following a linear mode of thinking, is the credo of schooling, a philosophy that took hold in the latter part of the era of industrialization, in the late 1800s. Use the formula or a chatbot to get the right answer. In contrast, educated learning teaches you how to think and problem-solve in a positive, inquisitive, and probing manner. You are *learning* to be a real estate developer and to address complicated issues in a creative, critical, and productive way. You are looking for *outliers* via the "education" approach versus the same old formula through "schooling."[8]

Responding to constant change and potential obstacles

We live in a disruptive age, unpredictable and tumultuous. Economic, social, and environmental factors are constantly changing and directly affecting real estate. These are either barriers or golden bridges to the future. It depends how you look at them and translate them into a positive future. Think of a coin toss. It has two sides—which one will you choose, and how will you use your choice to decide the outcome in your favour? Developers bring optimism and have a talent for avoiding roadblocks that tend to obstruct the success of their projects. Let's now look at some of the potential obstacles:

- **Health trauma and urban transformations.** The COVID-19 pandemic health and well-being emergency and associated lockdowns in 2020 to 2021 emptied out our cities. The pandemic made an estimated 30% of Canadian small businesses evaporate over two years. Following the pandemic, offices are converting to residential as more people work at home and the demand for office space shrinks. Digital shopping has also mushroomed.

- **Fiscal policy response.** Along with these economic shifts, inflation kicked in alongside the pandemic, with food prices doubling in some cases and restaurant prices doing the same. The government of Canada's fiscal response, in an effort to cool inflation, was to increase interest rates. Yet the combination of lack of housing affordability, income stagnation, and high interest rates placed a wet blanket over the real estate market in general. Potential buyers have pushed rental rates up as rental supply is limited, and these potential buyers waited for, among other things, interest rates to come down so they could enter a buyer's market.

- **Climate forces and benchmarking.** The changing climate is another disruptive and unpredictable force that affects real estate throughout North America. The National Centers for Environmental Information reported that billion-dollar climatic events have escalated from 4.5 in number from 1980 to 1999 to 18 between 2018 and 2022, and finally 23 in 2023 across the United States. The U.S. has sustained 323 individual weather and climate disasters that caused at least $1 billion in damages since 1980, for a combined cost of more than $2.2 trillion during that time frame.[9]

Climate resilience programs and policies are emerging and are now part of due diligence, not a peripheral topic for developers. Further, national, provincial, and municipal policies responding to climate change have added yet more costs to the housing market, with increased energy conservation and building code requirements. Plus, increased shoreline setbacks and flood construction levels have shrunk potential development footprints along shorelines.

- **Outmoded mortgage standards and an immigration tsunami.** So, how do we increase housing supply and decrease prices? The age-old criteria of Canada Mortgage and Housing Corporation (CMHC) to determine affordability was a benchmark of 30% of gross household income. This is unrealistic, for many people in Vancouver are spending up to 50% or more of their gross household income on shelter, while at the same time their disposable income has shrunk with inflation. Meanwhile, the federal government has set immigration targets (for permanent residents) at 485,000 in 2024, 395,000 for 2025, and 380,000 for 2026, inviting more than a million new residents to Canada.[10] For the first time ever, the Canadian population grew by one million people in 2023.[11] As a result, the external pressure on housing supply is increasing.

- **Housing construction not keeping up with demand.** While some developers argue that approvals timing and complexity is the major barrier, at the same time, shortages of skilled labour do not help more affordable housing production. The looming retirement of approximately 25% of those currently employed in construction over the next ten years is also a concern.[12]

Next-generation thinking

Let's think differently for a moment. There are some basic considerations as well as innovations that, if we integrate them, can radically change this seemingly unsolvable riddle of housing unaffordability.

- **Housing type, size, adaptability, and diversity.** There is a North American dream that persists (and in some circles is still believed to be an inalienable right) to own a four-bedroom home on a large single-family lot with a double car garage. What are we thinking?

    In reality, the townhouse is the new single-family home by affordability and design, featuring quality over quantity of space. Granted, North Americans must get used to more compact spaces and tighter living arrangements. We are not Europe but can aspire to their pedestrian-oriented city centres and efficient transit. Many of our post-war homes were 112 m^2 (1200 ft^2) in size. Why can't more of us live in the same arrangement with two to three bedrooms or live in a more compact townhouse that is supported by amenities for us and our families? The decision to downsize prioritizes quality over quantity, with savings in taxes, maintenance, and time to care for the property. The result is more money and time to spend on other, higher-priority items.

Prefabricated *passive housing* should also be considered to cut construction costs and create the most energy-efficient building envelope. Of European origin, passive housing requires less energy to heat and cool. The home design also significantly reduces greenhouse gases. This concept makes sense, but when I visited a passive house factory several years ago, because I was keen on the idea, I was surprised to learn that their costs were $600 per square foot for a custom model and $300 per square foot for the bare-bones version. This was not affordable in conventional terms at that time and costs are even higher today. We must find cheaper methods to create better and more energy-efficient homes.

Diversity of home types and sizes brings in an array of housing that is more inclusive and equitable. A townhouse and stacked townhouse configuration can include single-bedroom to four-bedroom homes, remembering that up to 40% of buyers are now singles, depending on location. Generally, cities have a higher concentration of singles compared to suburban and rural areas. Creating efficiencies, facilitating a greater sense of community, and sharing resources is the way of the future. The price of these units is normally much more affordable than detached single-family homes. Compact living lends itself to fewer cars, more mobility, and closer-knit communities if done well. Amenities can be shared and close by.

Figure 3. Next-generation thinking—it's not for us, it's for them. But who is "them" in our ever-changing world?

- **Housing tenure and suburban retrofit.** There is nothing wrong with renting an apartment or, better still, part of a home. In the new digital economy with digital nomads, renting is cool, flexible, and supports a more transitory lifestyle. It is not looked down upon anymore and it may be the trend of the future.

    Part of the future lies in converting single-family homes into multi-family homes. As it stands, many suburban communities are shrinking in population as families mature. Often, only two people are living in more than 232 m^2 (2500 ft^2)! The housing stock already exists but needs to be reshaped. My house and separate garage, for example, could become three to four living units, yet the form and character would look the same. Challenges often seen with increased density include parking for the additional vehicles associated with each unit as well as the physical and social infrastructure required to house additional residents.

A development colleague of mine just developed a home measuring 464 m^2 (5000 ft^2) in the Fleetwood area of Surrey, B.C., with two two-bedroom secondary suites in the lower level of 60 m^2 (645 ft^2). Each unit is generating more than $2000 per month in rental income. In another situation, in Chilliwack, B.C., a development manager I know purchased a new home with a suite and a coach house above the garage and is generating $6000 per month rental income from the two units. These two single-family house situations are multi-family homes where rental suites support the buyer as "mortgage helpers" or substantial revenue generators. Initially a mortgage helper, these investments can become transition space for children as they mature, then a haven for mom or dad in their single senior years, then a supplemental income to pension.

In Europe, renting a home for intergenerational families has been prevalent for decades. We must begin to regard renting in the same way. As I just mentioned, there seems to be an underlying bias towards buying your house, yet in most municipalities, such as Vancouver, only 50% or fewer residents own their homes. Even then, their bank owns a significant part of their home as the mortgage financer, especially in the case of younger to middle-age owners.

- **Mobility and proximity.** A growing population supports more transit and thus helps to make transit more convenient, more affordable, and more frequent. So, density done well, with ground-oriented units like townhouses and other multiple-family housing, can vastly improve community mobility and reduce the need for families to own multiple cars. Transit ridership is a challenge in Canada, especially in the sprawling suburban areas where most of us live. The myth that 80% of Canada is urban is simply that, a myth. In fact, according to extensive research and associated mapping by David Gordon of Queen's University, our metropolitan areas are mostly suburban, based on updated census data of 2021.[13]

- **Density, cost efficiencies, and social responsibility.** To quote from a recent Metro Vancouver Regional Planning report, "More compact development forms tend to reduce infrastructure costs on a per capita basis, support more efficient use of resources, and encourage more sustainable forms of transportation. However, the relationships between residential densities and public costs are complex; actual costs depend on the specific services and conditions, and local context."[14]

High density (high-rise apartments) does not necessarily result in the highest quality of life or in market fit. Granted that forward thinking on climate change advances higher density to cut greenhouse gas emissions. This may occur to some extent as more people live in a smaller space, near transit hubs, and more take transit, reducing their ecological footprint. But look at the vast vacant high-density cities in China or what happened in New York in the 1950s with the urban renewal projects—not success but social breakdown.

On the other hand, middle densities, which I prefer given a choice, or what is termed the *missing middle*—all those housing types between single-family housing and high-rise apartments—offer a whole range of housing types and can provide variety, diversity, inclusion, and quality of life. The missing middle normally includes townhouses, duplexes, triplexes, four-plexes, three- to six-storey apartments, and mid-rise apartments. I generally don't develop master plans for single-family housing anymore but rather for a mix of duplexes, triplexes, four-plexes, townhomes, rowhouses, and three- to six-storey apartments. Remember, there should be no increase in density without the accompanying amenities that support the greater population.

This kind of next-generation thinking provides compact and complete communities that fit various market demands. Also consider that high densities are riskier, since a developer can't build half a high-rise building, but phasing clusters of six townhouse units can work easily if the market demand changes.

- **Faster approvals.** For every developer, the topic of municipal and regional district approvals is an ongoing concern, since time delays cost more money in extended bank loans with variable interest rates. The internal process review itself and the amount of circulation and review by other provincial and federal agencies add layer upon layer of complexity and confusion, extending approvals and construction times to an average of up to five years or more in rezoning processes. It's too long a wait.

  In response, some municipalities are already harnessing artificial intelligence (AI) through the use of chatbots to expedite housing permit approvals. Combining this "blockchain" approach (fused history and connections) to ensure applications are comprehensively reviewed with less personal supervision and time is already being piloted by the City of Kelowna, B.C.[15] Add to AI the idea of outsourcing some applications to qualified project management professionals (PMPs) and this could further expedite project approvals, especially complex reviews.

- **Zoning, land use, and density.** One of my close planning colleagues suggested that we do away with antiquated zoning bylaws completely. Zoning regulations are over a century old and were enacted to separate what were then regarded as "nuisances," such as heavy industry and agriculture, from housing. Today, industry has largely cleaned up its act; only 15% is heavy industry anymore in many municipalities.

As we try increasingly to integrate and mix our living, work, play, and learning in more compact complete communities, zoning bylaws can become unduly complex. Municipalities need to replace outdated zoning bylaws, institute fewer zones, and look to the Official Community Plan for land use, density, and growth guidance.

Techniques to elevate your practice

- Strive to understand the bigger capital markets and how money flows.
- Learn the terms used by bankers and financial professionals.
- Try to consider the other side of the coin in thinking.
- Contemplate the alternatives.
- Adopt fast but conservatively.
- Bring multiple perspectives to idea generation.
- Hire the next generation to embed next-generation thinking.

Key take-aways

Take this opportunity to make a fresh start in your learning, exploring topics you want and need to know about. Business thinking, financial strategies, and macro- and micro-economics will challenge you at first, but then you will get comfortable with their language and confident to study each one of these topics in greater depth. This time will be well spent, for it gets you into the heads of investors, bankers, and economists. Your credibility will rise as you can then speak multiple business languages with ease.

To transform our lower-density cities and regions into more compact and efficient urban forms, we must fundamentally change our thinking about land use, zoning, housing types, and tenures. Otherwise, the same fundamental problems of lack of affordability, mobility, equity, and inclusion will continue to plague us.

With knowledge of the various influences that affect real estate development and the need to think ahead to the next buyer and next generation, let's examine how we develop the "idea" for the site. Further, a "place-driven" approach can help us understand the local community— what it needs and wants. Without this approach to site analysis, developers, who are often outsiders, risk running into community and political resistance.

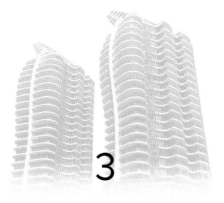

3

The Place-Driven Idea

Principle 3. Find the spirit of place to achieve success.

Imagination is greater than knowledge. Knowledge is limited. Imagination encircles the world.
—Albert Einstein

This chapter probes the beginning of any development process destined for success—the idea or concept. How is it generated and how can it be driven by place? We will explore the source and importance of the idea and how ten different elements can guide your place-driven agenda. Richard Florida, an American urban studies theorist focusing on social and economic theory, notes that the importance of "place" wins out over even income when it comes to choosing a city in which to live.[16] Understanding place—and its central role—is fundamental to the development process.

The development project idea starts in your imagination or by observing another project and translating that to your site. For me, a big idea can also be generated by facilitating a group conversation, since I tend to think and imagine on my feet, translating a word or words into a new direction. Frequently an idea also comes to me on my therapeutic runs, hikes, or bike rides, where different thoughts randomly emerge and solidify into a narrative that I scribble into my notes on my return, post-workout. Other creatives wake up with an idea. This is where our subconscious comes into play.

The idea for a real estate development may be an inspiration, thought, suggestion, or simply come from seeing another project. On the one hand, it can be as simple as another phase to an existing project or the redevelopment of an existing site. On the other hand, real estate development can be complicated and complex, such as a *mixed-use development* involving multiple phases and partners. But common to both less and more complex projects, certain questions emerge immediately.

- Is it the right idea to fit a site in a particular place?

- What is the land use—residential, commercial, institutional, industrial, resort recreational, or a mix?

- Who will buy the finished product? In the classic sense, is it a site looking for a land use or a land use looking for a site?

- Even more fundamentally, who will construct the project, and who will finance it?

- Is the concept likely to be approved by local government and under what circumstances?

- Will your financing partners regard the project as too risky? How can the project risk be minimized?

- Will the design of the building yield an acceptable profit that matches your goals?
- Will the buyers still be there when the building is at the pre-sale stage?

The match test

This last question is critical since it tests the core question: Why are you doing this development in the first place? When we start at the very beginning, this approach allows us to examine the full breadth of the potential project without an ingrained bias that could emerge from a defensive project manager halfway through a project. We need to articulate objective criteria that will shape our way forward and guarantee a good fit.

Whatever the development idea, ensure that the idea matches your personal or corporate goals and is realistic. For instance, imagine as an idea that you want to purchase a 2500-square-foot (232 m²) home in Whistler, B.C., but work in Vancouver. The purchase seems logical, since your family loves skiing and mountains, but is impractical from a commuting standpoint. Perhaps if you telecommuted three days a week, your choice of residence would make better sense, but Whistler to Vancouver is a long way to drive on a mountain highway. Maybe the realistic goal is to locate halfway or relocate your company.

On a corporate level, if your specialty is shopping centres and you are building a high-rise residential development on a shopping centre site, you must question the risk and experience factors in delivering the residential units on time and on budget. Is residential development your game, or should you bring in a partner with proven experience in this area?

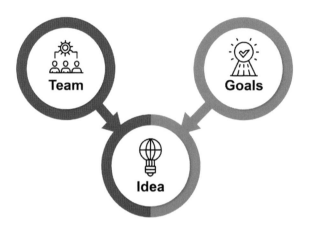

Figure 4. The idea is generated by team/individual thinking and is matched to specific goals.

Extending your development game

So, what if an opportunity emerges that is not your development specialty? What should you do? That is exactly what happened on one of my projects. The situation involved a perfectly located aging shopping centre ripe for redevelopment. The developer was well financed and focused on shopping centre redevelopment in Burnaby, B.C. The challenge was that this major development opportunity primarily involved residential high-rise towers that would infill the surface parking areas.

The developer chose to extend their expertise internally rather than partner for residential tower development, and that decision worked out well with the continuing market demand. Sometimes if you don't have the built-in, tested credentials, it is not only riskier but also difficult, if not impossible, to finance a particular project. In this case, the result was commendable and highly successful.

The bigger idea

The *bigger idea* in my lexicon is the idea that breaks the mould and creates a competitive edge, otherwise you will be doing the "same old stuff." In some markets, and for many developers, following the status quo is their norm. I like getting the edge on the competition by finding a unique piece of land that matches its use and general program, or, alternatively, finding something unique in fitting the use to the acquired land. I call it a "unique site signature."

This site signature does not have to be radical and, in fact, could be subtle, but it stands out and fits the specific buyer for the project. The next story illustrates my point. I recently completed a master plan concept for a site in Chilliwack, B.C., on First Nations lands. The master plan has a unique idea to respond to a volatile and sensitive market. My consulting group developed a flex-lot format that provides the opportunity to respond differently to changing demands. So, aren't lots fixed once you subdivide the property? Correct. But if the subdivision includes larger lots with flexible dimensions, then you can build different homes.

Lots that are either 25 metres (82 feet) or 32 metres (105 feet) deep fit single-family, duplex, triplex, and four-plex homes. The 32-metre lots allow coach houses over separate garages, all served by 7-metre (23-foot) lanes at the rear of the property. This lot configuration also permits a 3-metre (10-foot) front yard, versus the normal 6-metre

(20-foot) front yard, while optimizing density and diversity of housing units. The central area of this development has a community building connected to the rest of the community by "green streets," exclusively for pedestrians and bicycles, with street-fronting homes. Allowing flexibility in development permits that important "agility" component, discussed in chapter 1, that lets you change your product offerings with the changing market demand.

Ten elements to guide your place-driven agenda

We should be thinking at the speed of community, not the speed of business.
—Andy Yan[17]

In a recent discussion with my close friend and colleague David Witty, former dean of architecture at the University of Manitoba and senior fellow of urban design at Vancouver Island University, we talked about building "responsible and accountable" real estate projects. What emerged were the following ten keystones:

1. **Contributes to a sense of place.** The Romans had a Latin name for spirit of place—*genius loci.* It took the meaning of place as a geographic location to a new, metaphysical level. The concept was to capture the sense and meaning of the specific place.

   For example, I am working on a master development plan for an agricultural tourism destination just east of Calgary in Strathmore, Alberta, on the Trans-Canada Highway. This property has a unique and rich history as the

CPR Experimental Farm of Western Canada, and we want to recognize that history in the programming, design, and development of the site.[18] I believe that once you find that place magic, it acts as an authentic magnet and catalyst for site development, especially with millions of potential customers passing the site every year along the Trans-Canada Highway.

In shaping the Strathmore site around this authentic historical theme, my firm gained full community and council support for our *area structure plan* and received expedited approvals, with no delays.

2. **Respects and acknowledges contextual setting.** In a similar vein, the context should influence and shape the site. This concept of *context sensitivity* means that the surrounding land uses, roads, services, and environmental elements such as forests, streams, orientation, and views influence the site planning and should become part of the site development fabric. These are what I refer to as *site form-makers.*

   Neighbourhood conversations are important to provide the meaning of this context and what should be acknowledged and integrated into the site plan. These conversations not only inform the program, design, and development of the site but also build trust and support for your project in the community. In 2013, in Strathcona County, Alberta, my firm was doing a unique development saving the landform and created a natural drainage and amenity structure. A local physician living across the street from the site was adamantly against the project at the beginning, because he said it would destroy his community. Once we involved him in the process and he understood the full concept, including parks, trails, and tree buffers along his side of the project, he became our greatest supporter at council and phoned me to reserve one of the first lots for sale. Direct conversations, empathy, and understanding of context and neighbours' perspectives all matter.

3. **Contributes long term to community environmental and social aspirations.** A simple gesture like completing a publicly accessible trail system through your property (with limited hours for safety and security) can be a community contribution that gains broad support. Your interest in building community beyond your property lines is a genuine gesture that shows you are interested in the community and creates what I term *net environmental and community gains*, yielding a positive improvement in the environmental, economic, and social well-being in the community. In short, you as a developer should create improvements to the environmental, economic, and social aspects of the community as part of the development process. If you specify your contributions, community support is further assured, if other elements of the plan are not controversial.

4. **Reflects a philosophy of full-cost accounting.** Similarly, net community and environmental gain can be translated in some respects to the term *full-cost accounting*. This term means that the

economic, social, and environmental costs of the site development are taken into consideration. Normally, in line with the developer's interests, the economic analysis alone takes prominence, but more and more, the social and environmental cost-benefit analysis is becoming more prominent in the examination and review of the application by staff, council, and the community. Full-cost accounting takes in the fuller "public interests."

No one really cares about how much profit the developer is making, except the developer, investors, and the bank. Social and environmental matters trump economics from the community's viewpoint but may also have direct or indirect financial implications—especially in regard to timely support and approvals.

From 2009 to 2011 in Halifax, Nova Scotia, my firm worked on the largest redevelopment of a site in the city, located not far from Dalhousie University. We engaged ten interest groups in the community engagement process. As part of the process, we defined a *community benefit strategy* that included neighbourhood parking on site, public art, an internal block pedestrian connector, more affordable housing, and other benefits. We received unanimous approval by the city and regional governments in eleven months, with broad support from the community, which is rare for a project of this scale.

5. **Emulates best practices.** Best practices do not necessarily cost more. They provide better ways to do development that should be more efficient.

Make sure that you are part of the "leading edge," not the "bleeding edge." My experience is that tried-and-true methods, processes, and materials are worth adopting, but some are not tested and can be expensive. Be careful not to experiment without informed advice.

My wife and I are currently using advisors from the United States on our vacation home in Costa Rica regarding construction materials and techniques that are cost-effective, healthier, and environmentally sensitive. Energy self-sufficiency through micro-hydro on our creek and/or solar panels on our roof is one sustainability principle we are exploring, along with water conservation and natural cooling with ceiling fans, minimizing the requirement for air conditioning. Variables we are managing include availability of materials, cost, importation taxes, fabrication, complexity, and maintenance. Be careful, since untested foreign materials and/or techniques could create cost overruns or unnecessary complexity and maintenance requirements for your project.

6. **Respects and supports the public realm.** The *public realm* is everything outside the private property and includes publicly accessible space on private property. When you include the streets, parks, public parking, and other open space, the public realm makes up 40 to 50% of cities. It is what the community is interested in improving, since they control it with the city governments. The public realm has been largely disregarded in some cases as "residual space" and therefore neglected. That view is changing, with active

departments within cities advancing best public realm practices and asking developers to contribute. Direct contributions to adjoining streets and parks also improve developers' land values and potential sales.

See how contributing to the public realm can contribute to the value of your development project by reviewing my 2022 book *Public Realm: The New Makers Handbook.*[19] This book intends to inspire ideas, strategies, and standards for your next project that are the emerging best practices in public realm development.

7. **Permits aging in place and adaptation.** We should extend and make more flexible our housing, commercial, and industrial spaces. Most importantly, we must make room for residents to age in place rather than put further undue stress on our health care system. Research findings confirm that staying at home with support will help people lead happier, longer lives. Simple.

   We should also think of extending the life of our commercial and industrial spaces, while building in more flexibility to transform these spaces to other uses and configurations. Such practices lead to less waste and more recycling and up-cycling in terms of land use and density.

8. **Minimizes energy and water consumption during development and occupancy.** How do we reduce our consumption of energy and water, yet at the same time increase our livability and enjoyment? Our energy and water consumption in North America amounts to at least three to four times that of Europeans, and

there is so much waste. We should be conscious of our consumption through metering and pay for premium consumption if we are the ones responsible.

Low-flow toilets and faucets are a small step in the right direction. I was certainly more aware of my water consumption when I lived in Colorado, where I received a separate bill. In Canada we tend to combine our energy and water bills, making us less aware of our wastage and cost. We are in a sense spoiled by our perceived endless supply of energy and water. There appears to be no real sense of urgency or any negative incentives (disincentives, such as extra fees for surplus use) to prompt us to change our lifestyle.

Developers can play an important role in energy and water consumption. For instance, FortisBC is working with developers to install individual gas meters in apartment buildings so that each tenant is accountable for individual use. Conservation and reuse of water pro-grams (through cistern storage) in multi-family developments can help to reduce water demand. At the same time, proper passive solar orientation of buildings can optimize the sun's heat energy in winter, while reflective "cool roofs," extra overhangs, and appropriate landscaping, optimizing shade, can all help to reduce heat in the summer.

9. **Promotes and utilizes circular economy initiatives.** It is concerning to think that con-struction waste comprises 40 to 50% of our

landfill. How do we promote and utilize a no-waste concept in our wasteful world? Our attitudes must change with financial disincentives, and businesses and governments must make it easier for the construction industry to recycle. Requirements and municipal or regional district standards and regulations need to change. We are all part of the solution.

With a capable interdisciplinary team, my firm completed an award-winning eco-industrial area plan for the District of North Vancouver in 2004, more than twenty years ago. That was the first time I became familiar with the term *eco-industrial network* and the idea of the *circular economy.* In simple terms, during and after site development, everything is seen as a resource and is recycled, generating little or no waste. The by-products of development are recycled into value-added products or circulated as raw materials for other industrial processes. When was the last time you saw waste in a natural system like the ocean (except for human-generated plastic or other synthetic products)? In natural systems, everything is recycled. Traditionally, First Nations cultures also did not waste any of the resources they harvested. We should follow a similar path.

10. **Avoids formulaic design.** It is so easy to just "rinse and repeat," as the washing cycle goes. We have made a profit. Why not just repeat the cycle? That has happened in the extension of suburban sprawl over the past seventy years, leading to single-family homes, large lots, and

single-occupancy vehicles that drive everywhere and get nowhere in traffic gridlock. We have directly or indirectly subsidized this inefficient use of land through road building and service extensions. This approach to urban development has been our pattern language of success, but it is now leading to a dead end as Canada's infrastructure deficit is estimated to be between $110 billion and as much as $570 billion.[20] That is, to replace the infrastructure we have built, much of which is at the end of its fifty-year lifespan, will cost *at least* $110 billion.

So, we cannot build the same anymore, especially with the affordability crisis that faces many Canadians. Think developments that are smaller, higher quality, more compact, healthier, and have a higher sense of community. This is what was discussed in chapter 2. There is a huge opportunity here, and both consumers and municipal councils are helping to support these insightful changes. They must be sensitive to the fact that higher costs provide less affordable housing.

Figure 5. Place and people drive planning and a site's design program. Place, people, and program are interconnected.

Techniques to elevate your practice

- Find the *genius loci* (sense of place) for every project.

- Be future-oriented and design something unique but practical.

- Make your development healthy and as environmentally sensitive as possible.

- Think about creating an improvement to the surrounding neighbourhood.

- Free yourself, explore openly, and confine yourself only when necessary.

- Try to find a new niche or one that has already been tried successfully.

- Be the leading edge, not the bleeding edge (profit versus loss result).

Key take-aways

The idea or "bigger idea" for a development project has a conventional or opportunistic "site signature." You need to have the right team, and the project must fit your personal and/or corporate goals. The idea (or concept) has a sensitive and responsive application to the site. Ideally, the idea is somewhat flexible to a changing market. Alternatively, there is a straightforward development scenario with minimum risk and buyers at the front door. Finally, the idea is simply a beginning that should be verified through detailed pro forma (cash-flow) analysis (see next chapter) and continue to be refined throughout the development process.

If you find that sense of place or *genius loci*, you will find the unique site signature and competitive edge you are seeking. If you also aspire to best practices in context sensitivity, community needs, energy and water conservation, full-cost accounting, and full recycling with unique and flexible designs, you will create a great destination that is prosperous, thriving, inclusive, and enduring. Think long-term and build for 100 years, not 50 years—like rare visionary politicians—and consider the next generation of uses for your buildings and site.

Having weighed the importance of the place-driven idea, let's now combine place and business. The next chapter discusses understanding your buyer and marketing to their needs, as well as feasibility analysis to make sure there is a sound business case for the "idea." Without a detailed analysis of the market, a business plan with a supporting cash flow, and financial partners who support your project, the "place-driven idea" we've just discussed remains merely a dream.

4

Market, Feasibility, and Finance

Principle 4. Think market focus, return on investment, and financial analysis from the start.

> *Nationally, actual 2023 housing starts were down 7% in centres of 10,000 population and over, with 223,513 units recorded, compared to 240,590 in 2022 . . . Despite the national decline, actual 2023 housing starts were 5% and 28% higher than in 2022 in Toronto and Vancouver, respectively . . .*
> —Canada Mortgage and Housing Corporation, January 16, 2024
>
> *You don't know your buyer.*
> —Director of marketing

This chapter discusses three core elements of a successful real estate venture—market, feasibility, and finance. These three elements need to be aligned to make the original idea viable and durable in a highly volatile environment that can change abruptly. The sequence is important, since the market analysis will inform and ground your financial feasibility, and in turn shape the financing package for your partners and financial institution(s).

Know your market details and answer fundamental questions

Can you sell your real estate development product if you don't know exactly what your buyer wants? Is it the right location? What is the competition and how many units are they selling? What is the absorption of units (rate of purchase) trend in the market? At what comparable price are these units selling for? What do the buyers specifically want? These are the fundamental questions, and apparently you don't know your buyer! Time to analyze the market and get to know your buyer at a fine-tuned level.

As a true development rookie, I crafted *Marketing Guidelines for the Nu-West Community* in 1981 and presented them at the company's annual conference.[21] I knew little about marketing from experience, but I knew you had to consider the marketing process from the beginning of a project to sell your product effectively throughout the construction process, not when the show home was finally built. Sales revenue then accrues as early as possible, and advance sales build momentum and potential higher prices. In the end, the project is sold out earlier and at a higher price, assuming your promotion and sales generate more value and a sense of scarcity. Profit is maximized earlier with a more positive result, keeping in mind that this scenario assumes a rising market, otherwise the reverse may be true.

Market expertise from the outset

Market analysis has become a sophisticated process that should start near the beginning of the development process. Even during acquisition, it is astute to measure the site and its viability against the market. No question. You must match the development site and product type to the existing and emerging markets. A marketing specialist and market analyst should be at the table when you are developing the idea and then be an integral part of the team as you proceed.

Figure 6. Find your buyer. Who are they and what do they want?

Get to know the market for the specific real estate product you are developing. Whether it be housing, commercial, or industrial units, find out the characteristics of the market and how to be successful. Be careful with new markets that you don't understand or have experience with. If needed, take on a joint venture partner who can contribute outside expertise.

Test the market for new directions

A focus group and community surveys are excellent ways to test the market for new products and services that are part of the emerging buyer's profile. For the residential market, consider the following, plus more:

- The size of home and minimum number of bedrooms, considering that 40% of potential residents could be singles, depending on location.

- The need for a formal office space or even two flex spaces for home offices, the demand for which has ballooned since the pandemic along with more hybrid work arrangements.

- Secondary suites, or an additional lock-off suite, and/or an auxiliary development unit (coach house) on the lot.

- The garage for another use or flex use, with appropriate finishes and amenities, since more residents now require only one car, if any.

Develop comprehensive marketing and communications tools

Communication and engagement are radically changing. Chat platforms spread a well-conceived communication piece in minutes. The reach is then thousands or more. Develop a careful brand that stands out and has a signature attention-grabber. Provide incentives for audiences to dig deeper. Show you care about their needs. Design exclusive invitations to a sales centre to create a magnet for more to attend.

Use digital media platforms, from Facebook (older generation) to X or LinkedIn, to promote events, unique offerings, and special programs. You need to hook your buyers' attention within 5 to 10 seconds online or they are tracking something elsewhere. Sales events with free ice cream or children's activities, or a website with an eye-catching home page can make the difference. Follow-ups with new information on pricing and potential custom-priced sales packages can bring buyers back. Ultimately, it is the person-to-person relationship that closes the deal in the end with the right price, however, that price is based on sales elements, conditions, and financing.

Choose the right data to shape market strategy

National housing market numbers may show a trend. Numbers don't lie, some say. Yet are they the right numbers and are they being fairly represented? Most Canadians are suspect of numbers and economic analysis, since figures can be manipulated or carefully selected to create a misrepresentation of the facts (exaggerated and/or lacking specific context).

For example, what if I were to say, "We have an affordability crisis, and no one can afford to buy a new house." This statement may be true from one perspective, if you assume the City of Vancouver market, with the average single-family house costing $1.5 million and the average family income at $80,000 per year. But when you review townhouse and apartment prices in the Greater

Vancouver area, like Langley City, you come to a slightly different conclusion, since properties tend to be cheaper but may still be relatively unaffordable compared to family incomes. In our complex world, you must compare apples to apples in the same location (comparable numbers) from both the macro-and micro-economic perspectives discussed earlier in chapter 2.

So how do we analyze the market data and choose the right data in this data-rich world?

Big data and selection

We are overwhelmed by thousands of data bits every day. Where your focus goes, so goes your energy. To avoid overload, I limit my social media exposure and select certain streams and information sources. I try to use trusted sources like rennie intelligence (rennie.com/intelligence) or MLA Canada (mlacanada.com). It is amazing how "paper" newspapers have become outmoded, but you can still find reputable publications online like the previous sources that represent current market trends. Be careful of your sources and compare data. Bigger development companies often use their own trusted data or have consultants who keep them up to date. Contractors and builders are the best sources for current construction costs, since they are buying materials and using labour every day. Alternative sources of construction costs include Altus Group (altusgroup.com) and Statistics Canada (150.statcan.gc.ca).

It is one thing to examine past and current data and then estimate trends in this ever-changing time. But how can we approach the numbers behind development to achieve optimum results in guiding our business? Let's start as the beginning with our own numerical analysis framework, so we don't get confused by all the numbers and information "noise." This noise is often overwhelming, so the key is to be selective and focus on your needs.

Pro forma cash-flow projections

All projections tend to be wrong. The question is, by how much? We might be wrong but not by much if we do our homework well. That said, major deviations and wrong assumptions can lead to misleading information and overly optimistic or pessimistic views that are unrealistic and, more importantly, unreliable.

The primary tool for developers in doing financial projections is the *pro forma*, a cash-flow projection for a project over at least several years. A pro forma is normally modelled using Microsoft Excel or a customized real estate software program. The Altus Group's ARGUS EstateMaster is one of the leading property development feasibility, appraisal, and project cash-flow management software tools.

In the pro forma standard set-up there are revenue, hard cost and soft cost categories, and then profit measurements that collectively shape the basic format. These costs include construction *hard costs* to improve the site and building as well as *soft costs*, including consultants, financing costs, development fees, and other non-construction but directly related development costs. Pro formas vary based on the type of project and the depth of the analysis. An economist friend of mine used to "collect" pro formas from various developers because he was working on many different residential projects with complex mixed-use pro formas. These pro formas gave him various formats, content, and market absorption (sales timing) assumptions that he could compare to his own.

But assessing feasibility usually starts out with a *back-of-the-envelope analysis*, where the basic numbers are listed to determine a viable purchase price and potential profit. The equation is in its simplest terms: *revenue minus costs = profit*. Then the gross profit can be converted to a percentage by dividing the gross profit by revenue or costs to determine simple (static) *return on investment* (return on revenue or return on cost over one year). The industry norm requires a return on cost of between 15 and 18%. Return on revenue can be slightly lower, at 12 to 15%. Higher risk, higher return. Lower risk, lower return.

As the project proceeds, each of the subsequent pro formas becomes more detailed, with more refined cost and revenue line items as well as the extension of annual cash flows over the project's time frame up to 10 to 20 years, especially if the project is retained as a leased and/ or rental property incorporated into the multi-year cash-flow analysis.

In addition, to determine the viable land price at the beginning of the project, a *residual land value* analysis should be completed. In elementary terms, all the variables of revenue and cost are included as well as expected profit to determine the estimated land price that you can pay. If the projected land price is *too high,* that will lower the acceptable profit (return on cost or revenue). If the projected land price *is lower than expected,* that will increase profit.

To give one example, I was reviewing pro formas for a development company some years ago. The peculiar thing about the set-up was that there was no "bottom line," literally no return on revenue or cost at the bottom of the pro forma. When I completed the calculations, I noticed a return of 5 to 8% on revenue, well below the industry average, and these projects were in the medium- to high-risk categories. These projects were marginal at best.

I questioned the senior executive vice-president and president about my concerns. Both of them tended to skirt the issue, since their company received a sizable management fee to manage the project. My conclusion was that they were satisfied with their management fees and chose not to emphasize the return on revenue or costs. But investors might think differently. Remember, if you don't have a cushion in your return on investment that is adequate, if some of the costs escalate or the revenue projection decreases, you can easily lose money on the project—even with a normal contingency of 5% on costs.

Key market and quantitative analysis questions

Let's start with the fundamentals, as mentioned above. The following twelve questions start to capture the essence of the numbers side of your financial analysis. Even at the beginning of due diligence, there should be a real possibility that the project is feasible and profitable. Keep in mind that your investors and bankers will also need to endorse your proposal, otherwise you will be out of luck and capital to fund the project.

1. Does the market in your municipal area or regional district have a demand for your specific type of housing or other land use and how much is estimated (**demand numbers**)?

2. What is the competition and timing of delivery (**supply numbers**)?

3. Is the **price of the property** affordable based on your pro forma analysis (or can you renegotiate the price and terms)?

4. Are there any **environmental or physical aspects** of the site that could significantly add to revenue (e.g., views and orientation) or add to costs (e.g., soil contamination or environmental setbacks)?

5. Do the **revenue potential** and ranges still allow the projected minimum profit?

6. Do you have **trusted sources for your costs and revenue** depending on the timing and needs (e.g., Class D, C, B, and A construction costs— see next section and chapter 8)?

7. What are the **estimated costs** and potential variations?

8. Does the profit provide a range of 12 to 15% **return on revenue or** 15 to 18% **return on cost**?

9. Have you incorporated some **sensitivities on interest rate changes** as well as other sensitivities, like revenue and costs?

10. Have you used more complicated **internal rate of return (IRR)** or **net present value (NPV) calculations** to further test the timing of acquisition, sales, and/or disposition of the property over several years?

11. What is the **timing of approvals** and how will it impact the cost of the project?

12. Can you **defer the acquisition** of the property based on approval of rezoning or other associated approvals (e.g., joint venture with the property owner)?

Different numbers at different times in the process

Question number 6 above addresses the level of detailed costing at different times in the process. The costing details increase with each stage of design. For clarity:

- *Class D cost estimate*—normally done at schematic design stage
- *Class C cost estimate*—at design development stage
- *Class B cost estimate*—at building permit stage
- *Class A cost estimate*—at tendering for construction

As the project advances in detail and specifications, so too do the costs to provide added certainty, as developers fine-tune their budgets and allocations to different development phases. A similar process applies to the revenue side as the project gets closer to construction. Constant monitoring of costs and revenue leads to a more accurate pro forma as the project progresses.

Exploring alternatives and different scenarios

Just like cost estimates, the design and unit profiles could change through the design process to respond to market preferences, thereby affecting revenue and costs. Both the revenue and costs are sensitive to changes. If the revenue increases in line with costs, then the return on investment will be similar or the same. If revenue remains flat while costs increase, your return on investment will decrease, unless the contingency in the soft costs can absorb any change orders and cost increases.

Checking your assumptions

Always go back to your assumptions, including your quantitative and qualitative goals for the project, to ensure they are in alignment. Be critical in your analysis. Pay attention to detailed findings. Working the numbers behind real estate development is critical to success and support from investors and bankers.

I was told once that detailed pro formas are only for the bankers. I was somewhat surprised. Maybe this is true for very detailed financial analysis, but the pro forma is also a tool for project budgeting and funding, so developers have certainty but also a degree of flexibility. Financial analysis is one way to measure success. However, ultimately it is also the *qualitative* assessment of the project and its sense of community that create enduring value. After all, we are not designing for robots, but for humans. Things such as emotion and experience cannot be quantified easily or sometimes even quantified at all.

In all real estate projects, there is a need and desire for external financing. Investors are partners in development because they have a stake in the outcomes. The most common reason for financing is that the project is too big for the developer to provide all the equity (cash) to complete the land acquisition and construction. Chapter 6 discusses partners in more depth, but here the discussion centres on financing.

Conventional first mortgage and chartered banks

If the developer provides only 25% of the project equity (cash injection by the developer) and benefits from the balance being provided by a bank, they can leverage their money with other money to make a higher return on investment. This concept is called *positive leverage* (the return on equity is higher, with lower investment requirements). This lower equity requirement also allows the developer to do more projects and spread out their retained cash in smaller quantities. As a general rule, the larger banks lend up to 75 to 85% on construction financing and 50 to 60% on land acquisition, since the latter is riskier.

The banking business is by its nature conservative. Bankers generally frown on progressive, outside-the-box ideas, unless they have been market tested. That is why there are often conservative (risk-averse) higher interest rates with the larger chartered banks in Canada. The Bank of Canada lowered its key interest rate by 50 basis points to 3¾% on October 23, 2024, "to support economic growth and keep inflation close to the middle of the 1% to 3% range."[22] The interest rate has cumulatively been reduced by 125 basis points since the easing began in June 2024 and this was the fourth consecutive reduction. Interest rates are on a downward trend. Inflation rates have declined, with expectations for a continuing lower rate trend. But the former days of nominal interest rates are improbable in the short term, especially in this unstable geopolitical time.

Second mortgage or mezzanine financing

To further reduce their investments, developers also seek out investors and secondary financing. Instead of an equity requirement of 25% of the entire project, the developer reduces their investment to 15%, and therefore increases their leverage. At the same time, the cost of money increases with secondary financing (interest rate is higher), because the risk is increased for the second mortgage holder. If the project runs into trouble, the first mortgage holder is the first to receive any proceeds. The second mortgage holder follows. Secondary financing can be done through a bank or a private placement finance company.

Investors

Developers can also seek private investors to reduce their cash investment. These investors take an equity position in the venture or are part of an investment pool. Their returns can vary drastically but are normally now in the range of 9 to 12% return, based on the risk and type of project. If the returns on investment are higher, be suspicious of the investment, since the proposal starts to border on or exceed the developer's conventional parameters of 15 to 18% return on cash investment.

In summary, the stack of money or *capital stack* usually consists of development equity, investors, primary financing, and, sometimes, secondary financing, with the percentage interest varying and the interest rates and return on investment also varying, depending on the project and location.

Developer's covenant and investment criteria

Here are the criteria that banks and financial institutions use to measure the investment quality of a development project.

- **Quality of the project.** The location, type, and characteristics of a development are important to any financial group. Does the property have existing cash flow? Does it require *rezoning*? What is the proven demand in the marketplace for sale, rent, or lease? What is the *loan to value ratio (LVR)* in the requested financing terms?[23]

- **Potential returns.** What is the projected return on investment based on return on cost or revenue, internal rate of return (IRR), and/or net present value (NPV)? These financial projections should include possible medium-term cash flow and disposition of the asset customized to the project.

- **Quality and value of the client.** This criterion is important as the real estate developer's *covenant.* That is, the developer's reputation, experience, net worth, and assets largely determine the bank's comfort level with the financing.

- **Proven ability to deliver.** Related to the previous criterion, the developer's experience in this area and type of development is seen to affect their potential for success.

- **External market, timing, and term sheet.** Many of the large banks and other funders need approval from their head office in Toronto, so national trends affect financing, as does timing. The eventual offer normally comes in the form of a *term sheet*, which states the interest rate, term, and other conditions associated with the offer to finance the property.

Techniques to elevate your practice

- Mine data to find out what your buyers want.
- Visit other competitors' project sites and find out more.
- Develop marketing narratives that match the market.
- Put yourself in the buyer's or renter's shoes to understand their perspectives.
- Verify your assumptions with three sources.
- Complete a financial sensitivity analysis based on both optimistic and pessimistic assumptions to reflect different potential outcomes.
- Make sure you are presenting the right numbers.
- Check the numbers with trusted second-party or third-party sources.
- Know your lenders and establish clear communication channels to build a trusting relationship.
- Ensure that your pro forma is conservative and matches the successful return-on-investment measures.

Key take-aways

Always review the numbers or numeric analysis from several perspectives. Test your figures and look at optimistic, pessimistic, and realistic scenarios. This rigour will give you a balanced view and help you prepare for any criticism or questioning from investors and bankers.

The pre-sale or direct sale are both revenue. That generates profit. Without sales, and the associated revenue, you simply will not be financed and reach your development goals. Develop a marketing and sales team that strives to know the market and constantly adjust their strategies. Your lenders are your partners. Know them well and communicate on a continuing basis. Careers depend on it.

This chapter stressed understanding the market and doing a feasibility analysis to see whether your product would sell and at what price. Then we closely examined the costs and completed a cash-flow analysis to see if the project was viable. In other words, the project met at least the 12 to 18% rate of return on cash or revenue (noting these measures may vary depending on project risk and risk tolerance). These projected returns make it attractive enough to proceed to the next step, from a preliminary analysis.

The next part of the book addresses all the aspects of site development, from site review and testing through to partnerships, refinement, approvals, and construction in further detail. Throughout this process, one essential practice connects all these aspects together—constant refinement and improvement.

PART 2

SITE
DEVELOPMENT

5

Site Review and Testing

Principle 5. Let the site speak to you.

> *Seeing is very difficult, so you must choose*
> *what you see and let the rest go.*
> —Jordan B. Peterson

Now comes our true due diligence, where we review and test the site. This is both a quantitative and qualitative process in which aspirations meet site opportunities and constraints. Measuring twice or three times—that is, seeing, reading, and confirming—is necessary to truly confirm especially sensitive areas of the site and its context.

How do you let the site speak to you and really test the site so you are comfortable with the realistic and predictable outcomes? Put your boots on the ground. See and experience the site several times. In our Google Earth–oriented society and digital age, sometimes we tend to underestimate the site itself. All the site elements and their context inform the site use and architectural responses; these elements are the real form-makers.

The site planning and architectural site testing allow us to answer three crucial questions that determine *where* and *what* we can build on the site:

1. **What portion of the site can be developed?** If it is a larger site, referred to often as a master planned community with multiple uses, the general rule is that approximately 50 to 60% of the site can be developed when roads, existing significant trees, open space (environmental and park), and required setbacks/easements are considered. The 50 to 60% development capacity may be rather surprising, especially when developers pay for 100% of the site. At the same time, other sites can be almost fully developed (say, 80 to 90%), since they are already subdivided lots with road or street frontage in place and without site elements such as streams, trees, or other environmental features that may limit development.

2. **How much can be developed?** The next question is, how much volume or density can be developed on the site, under current or anticipated municipal or regional district regulations? The standard density measurement in urban areas is *FSR (floor space ratio)* or *FAR (floor area ratio),* which measure the volume of the building compared to the area of the site. For example, 1.0 FSR means that one floor of building can be built on the entire area of the site. Normally, if you can build, let's say, 50% of the site (excluding access, streets, parks, and other open space), 1.0 FSR means you can build

two floors on half of the site. Commercial or industrial are normally measured in FSR or FAR, with lot coverage and setbacks to further define what and where building is permitted.

The other density measurement in more suburban or rural areas is *UPA (units per acre)* or *UPH (units per hectare,* a 2.471 x UPA factor, since there are 2.471 acres in a hectare). These units normally mean single to multiple housing units per acre or per hectare. In standard terms, density of 4 to 10 units per acre relates to single-family housing; 11 to 20 units per acre relates to townhomes or attached housing units; and above 20 units per acre relates to apartment dwellings. These measures may vary.

3. **What kind of land uses are permitted?** The specific land use permitted on the site and allowable density (existing or anticipated) is important in determining the value of the site and market potential. If an owner wants a new use or density increase, they normally require a rezoning outside allowable limits, which requires additional time, review, and resources. The exact process and approval requirements are discussed later in the book, in chapter 7.

To help answer all three questions, refer to the municipality or regional district's Official Community Plan and its zoning bylaw. The OCP sets out the growth parameters and locations (land use "designations"), while the zoning bylaw contains specific "zones" and accompanying regulations, including density, setbacks, height, and building coverage.

The natural site elements and those that are built must be observed in real time and balanced in your site review. For instance, you can't experience the feeling of an immense maple or cedar tree and its shade by virtual camera or drone. Get out there and walk as well as photograph the site. The site soils, prevailing winds, watercourses, low-lying areas, vegetation, wildlife corridors, microclimates, views, and adjoining uses all help to inform your bigger ideas, especially in a rural context, where open space is more important than density. There could be context influences at play too. The site may be just a small puzzle piece of the larger watershed (drainage basin), and normally a small piece of one or more First Nations' traditional territory. These bigger forces and shapers at play outside the site boundaries influence the uses, site development capacity, and development form and character.

In a more urban context, where *redevelopment* is the scenario, then the site context (adjoining uses and other elements) comes into play in a big way. What are the uses and heights of adjacent buildings? How do you access the site and connect to the neighbourhood? What is important to the neighbourhood to conserve? It could be as simple as a widened sidewalk or a small-scale community park. The surrounding community doesn't care about the interior designs of the units; they care about how their community will be improved through publicly accessible places (the public realm) and how the development will be integrated.

Most importantly, talk to the locals and get their views on things. Informal conversations can reveal things that you cannot see due to the season, time, or hidden nature of certain constraints or opportunities in developing the site. Take, for example, a concealed underground fuel tank, the peak-hour traffic, or the seasonal winds or flooding that affect the area.

A monk's careful observation
in our nation's capital

My stepbrother Joey Kroeger shared a story about the construction of the Japanese Zen Garden on the roof of the Canadian Museum of History (formerly Civilization), on the Ottawa River in Gatineau, Quebec, almost thirty years ago, in 1995. As recorded by the head of the design team, Don Vaughan, "The theme of the garden, as expressed by its creator, Shunmyo Masuno, is Wakei No Niwa, which means to know and respect the history, culture and spirit of the Japanese and Canadian people, and to foster harmony between all nations."[24]

As the prime contractor, Joey was responsible for picking up Masuno, a Zen Buddhist monk from Japan, at the Ottawa International Airport. When he reached the arrivals area, he found the monk in his traditional garments waiting. The monk requested they go to the site where the rocks for the Japanese garden would be extracted. They went to the rock quarry, and the visitor inspected the various rocks there.

After some time, and patiently, Joey said he could drop off Masuno at the hotel downtown and pick him up again in the morning. To Joey's amazement, the monk simply thanked Joey and said he could leave and pick him up in the morning at the rock quarry. Nothing more was said. Joey finally understood that this dedicated monk wanted to deeply observe the site and choose the right boulders that best fit the site.

Masuno stayed overnight at the rock quarry, meditating on the best rocks for the Japanese garden. It could be said that it was a metaphysical/spiritual process to decide on the right rocks. Although this example may be slightly unusual, it reveals the underlying importance of knowing the materials and your site intimately.

You don't necessarily have to go to the extent of meditating overnight on the site, but the story of the monk shows how important your site is and how added features, such as large boulders, are instrumental in shaping the design. I am experiencing the same process in Costa Rica, where my wife and I plan to build a vacation home. We visit the site frequently to design and site our house to gain maximum views, take advantage of ocean breezes, and optimize solar orientation. We want the best housing site and layout on our 1.2-hectare (3-acre) property.

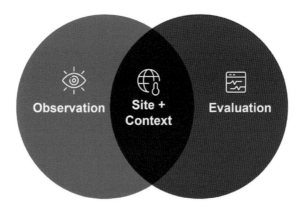

Figure 7. Both careful observation and stringent evaluation go into testing a site and its context.

One more story. While I was working at the City of Vancouver in the 1990s, I reviewed a downtown development application where the proposed landscape plan replaced all the existing street trees. In visiting the site, I verified that some of these street trees were healthy and vigorous. The proposed replacement of trees puzzled me, so I phoned the landscape architect in charge of the plan. He simply said that the budget had not allowed a site visit. I met him on site 30 minutes later and we resolved the matter by retaining the healthy trees and complementing them with further tree planting.

Take a closer look through multiple lenses

So, you think your development proposal works! You are in love with the proposal. Could it be you are wearing rose-coloured glasses that filter out any negative factors? You are wrapped up in the excitement of an idea and a site. You are selling the idea and merits of the site daily. But what if you have missed something? Do you want to be part of the leading edge or that bleeding edge (profitless project) that we already talked about? You might have missed something crucial that could undermine the entire project.

Balancing optimism with reality is a crucial part of real estate development. As one of my colleagues says, "There is always something." Is that *something* an issue that can be readily resolved? Or is it an issue requiring a strategy to resolve it that leads to success? This situation is what is called "risk." You need to reduce risk as much as possible.

Watch for sharks in the water

To manage risk is to be aware of what could happen and manage against the negative results. Picture yourself going into the Pacific Ocean off the Island of Maui for an offshore swim early in the morning after a rainstorm, by the mouth of a river with numerous sea turtles around. Not a good idea, especially with it being prime time for tiger sharks feeding. The risk is too high, and the environmental and time factors are against you. I would recommend swimming lengths in the hotel's pool instead. You just eliminated the risk.

Yes, there are also sharks in the development industry, to use the same metaphor, and they can be economic, social, or environmental factors. These are the multiple analytic lenses you should look through and they should not be rose-coloured. Each of these factors on face might not be threatening, but when tempered by specific regulations, political forces, or community bias can be highly toxic to a project. You need to look at each in depth, as described in the "Acquisition Comprehensive Checklist" (due diligence checklist) in my earlier book, *New Pathways to Approvals.*[25]

This comprehensive due diligence is required before you confirm the purchase of a property. This due diligence period is normally 30 to 60 days, depending on the strength of the real estate market. You can lengthen this period if the vendor is willing to take an "option" (paid extension) on the property, which is difficult to negotiate in a hot market. It is important to do a good job of this analysis. If you miss something, it could surface and potentially endanger the project later in the development process.

- **Do your homework.** My real estate development professor once told me: "He who does his homework the best, is best prepared." That credo has stayed with me to today, for when I have not completed my homework for real estate or a related project, the outcomes have been unpredictable or, even worse, undesirable. As an example, I come well prepared to a project meeting with a detailed pre-circulated agenda, fully informed with a comprehensive review of the facts and background on the project, an associated list of questions, and/or a well-conceived series of ideas that have been documented in digital and copied form and all been pre-rehearsed.

- **Measure twice and cut once.** Some years ago, I heard a story in which a critical error was made in haste to close a real estate deal. The individual assumed the architect's estimate on the site yield of 39 townhouse units was correct. After a cursory few hours' review, the individual put down a non-refundable deposit of $1 million. The following day, he found out from another colleague that the consultant had underestimated the watercourse development setback at 15 metres (49¼ feet) rather than the required 30 metres (98½ feet). This difference decreased the development yield from 39 units to 30 units and thereby erased the potential profit from the project. Only the courts could get the developer's $1 million back now. A potentially costly lesson emerged: Where there is a stream in British Columbia, verify the required setback through legitimate sources and confirm that measurement twice, not once.

- **Analyze physical, social, and economic factors.** Let's step back now and look at the most important factors, without becoming too consumed by an in-depth technical analysis. Sometimes you miss the big things in doing the detailed analysis. What is curious about real estate is that economic analysis tends to dominate the feasibility study when in fact it is the social and physical factors that can make or break a project. In brief, some of the examination includes:

◎ *Physical.* Location and orientation, flood level, soils, trees, wildlife, contamination, streams, microclimate, wetlands, and infrastructure location and capacity.

◎ *Social.* History and First Nations, legal matters (ownership, rights, public rights-of-way), policy issues, local support, and politics.

◎ *Economic.* Valuation, employment, immigration, market trends, land use, timing of approvals, revenue, costs, profit, depth of target market and competition, financing sources, and partners.

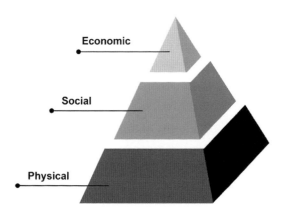

Figure 8. Multi-dimensional site review and testing uncovers physical, social, and economic conditions related to a project.

Test assumptions again

What are the litmus tests to ensure that a real estate development does not change colour? That is, change from black (profitable) to red (unprofitable). There are at least the three variable lenses (physical, social, and economic) already mentioned, but each can be considered again or in a more refined manner, and each of these lenses translates into a return-on-investment calculation. Always remember, as we already discussed, that the pro forma (future cash flow) is a guiding light that will vary but hopefully will be close to the market demands. Now let's look more closely at those physical, social, and economic factors so important to a development's viability.

1. **Physical value.** Think of the physical aspects of the site as form-makers for dollar value. For example, if the soil needs replacement or is unstable and requires piles to construct a foundation, then the whole "normal" changes to "abnormal" conditions and with premium costs. Each of the spatial and quality factors affects several variables, including land use, density, and development capacity. Ensure that these basic physical characteristics of the site are carefully assessed.

2. **Social support.** In simple terms, if the community, the municipal or regional government, the provincial or federal government, or special interests do not support your project, then significant delays and even denials could be the outcome. If the property does not have to be rezoned or require an Official Community Plan

amendment, then the risk is reduced significantly regarding timing of approvals, requirements for public review, and certainty. So, again, meeting with the important decision-makers, analyzing the policies, and knowing the regulations are routes to success.

3. **Economic viability.** Are the costs increasing or decreasing, and do you have construction costs from a current trusted source in the city or area? Can you verify costs with local builders? Local costs are important; construction costs in the resort community of Whistler, for instance, can be double those in Vancouver due to the more limited supply and availability of labour and materials. This situation results in a construction estimate that can increase from $400 to $800 per square foot or higher for a single-family home, depending on quality and finishes. The type of development, location, and sub-markets will all make a difference. Regional variations across Canada can also be drastic. Better to be on the conservative side rather than too optimistic in your projections, for your banker will want to know if you did a market study that will divulge supply, demand, revenue, costs, and competition.

Spread risk and have an exit strategy

What if your site testing doesn't work? Time is ticking, and highly leveraged developers are constantly depleting their resources by paying out loans monthly, especially if the approvals process is delayed. As referenced in chapter 1, this situation can be referred to as *negative leverage*. Carrying costs can quickly or slowly kill a project. Banks are conservative and tend to limit their exposure in a market sensitive to interest rate fluctuations. During the 2008 to 2009 real estate crisis, many Canadian banks did not fund land purchases, since land is the riskiest investment. However, zoned land with income properties in a prime location brings much more certainty, plus cash flow to help weather any economic downturn.

An exit strategy is always a good thing to have, as part of a develop-and-hold strategy or development-and-sell strategy. As you know, the market can trend downward fairly quickly, and what are we to do? To reiterate, if you are building an apartment building, you cannot build half a building and stop, but if you are building townhouses, you could build them in a phased strategy and buy additional land as you proceed.

Building value at every step

In extreme cases, you should plan to sell a portion of the property to generate capital to reduce the relative risk. The key here is to build value at every step of the development process. In this instance, further appraisals could then increase the sales value and the return on the initial investment. So, how do you accomplish this result? Let's look at three methods of increasing value and spreading risk.

- **Rezoning.** Changing the zoning of a property creates a "land lift" in the property value, as your land use has changed and/or density permissions have increased. The land value (appraised value) increases as the amount of floor space and/or number of units increases and therefore the saleable area increases. The land value can significantly increase in situations where the increase in density far exceeds the existing use (e.g., rezoning from a single-family zone to a high-density residential zone).

- **Joint venture.** When you enter into a joint venture, your equity (cash) outlay is less, since you normally share in-kind (vending in the property) or in a cash contribution. That is also why developers spread out their equity to more than one property—to decrease their risk and increase returns on their reduced cash insertion in each deal. It is another way to *leverage* their cash contributions.

- **Secondary or mezzanine financing.** As we have seen in chapter 4, this secondary financing reduces the amount of cash (equity) the developer requires to contribute to the project financing. The downside is that this secondary financing has an interest rate premium.

Techniques to elevate your practice

- Walk your site with your consultants before you execute the purchase contract, as part of the due diligence period.

- Visit the site more than once (during a different time of the day or on the weekend) to observe both physical and social patterns (wind, orientation, and current uses).

- Ensure that you review, through special consultants, the policies and standards that govern development of the site and adjoining sites.

- Confirm existing and emerging land use policies with the informed planner and engineer at the municipality or regional district.

- Look for factors that can undermine the development process or the projected costs.

- Find the "red flags" or deal-breakers, such as lack of municipal or community support for rezoning, land contamination, or excess off-site improvement costs.

- Build value at every step.

- Exit if necessary and make a profit in the process.

Key take-aways

You might have reviewed different parts of the site, but a detailed review entails things that you can't see. Always measure twice and cut once to ensure you received the right information and that the information is current. The three lenses you use to analyze your proposal should include physical, social, and economic reviews that take a deep dive especially into aspects of the sales pitch that are suspect. Talk to people directly to verify all information.

This chapter identified the need to know your site and its development capabilities thoroughly. Without in-depth knowledge of your site through local, experienced professionals, all can be lost due to a simple oversight. Now, with this firm grounding and a comprehensive development package in hand, it is time to approach your financial partners and take your project to the next stage.

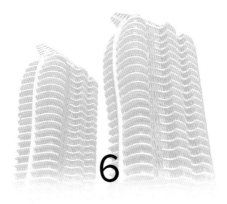

6

Partners and Elevation

Principle 6. You cannot go it alone.

> *Partnering is a key to primary greatness. Unless we are willing to work together to sacrifice our pride of ownership, of our ideas, or our image, we will not meet the ever-growing demands of the marketplace.*
> —Stephen R. Covey

Who said you can't do development alone? You got here by yourself, didn't you? My "principled" advice might be humbling words for both a rookie and an experienced real estate developer. What I mean by "You cannot go it alone" is that you need the support of your investors, banker, approval authority, community, and municipal or district council to proceed with your project. In addition to this core group, your building contractor and consulting group need to be among the cheerleaders that support and promote the project.

This chapter brings your financial partners into the project for their insights and refinements. The banks and investors, as we will learn, contribute different perspectives to the project that can make it that much more viable and resilient.

Partners in real estate development

To partner up is advice that comes from experience. In this complex world, especially in real estate development, trying to proceed on your own is riskier and unnecessary. Obtain advice from trusted colleagues who will have a stake in the project, for the core group of investors and bankers have their own goals and investment criteria that will refine the project proposition. Certain measurements, like time to complete, and pro forma assumptions such as absorption of units, sales prices, hard and soft costs, loan to value ratio, and return on investment are all required in your proposal to your financial partners. (See chapter 4 and the glossary for definitions and clarification.)

When deals go sideways

What if a real estate project sours, especially in a downward market where demand decreases and real estate prices decrease? Taking two recent actual case studies, let us look at two properties, both well located, and one with a significant cash flow from a building on the property. The developers ran into financial challenges as interest rates climbed, construction costs inflated, and the market demand cooled. The developers defaulted on their interest payments and the banks (primary lenders) foreclosed on both properties.

In both cases, the properties were listed for sale by the first-mortgage bank and second-mortgage joint representative and had potential offers to be finalized. In both cases, their loan to value ratios left a significant buffer in case something went wrong. The properties had development permits and had completed rezoning or were well along in the process.

But in one case, the purchase offer was barely half the appraised value! In addition, the primary lender had an interest premium requirement (an increased interest rate on the loan in the interim period since the loan default). The proceeds from the sale covered the funding from the primary lender and accrued interest, but less than half of the secondary lender funds. Both funders were not willing to wait for a more acceptable offer to all parties.

At the same time, in the other case, the primary lender was patient, since their interest costs were covered by the rental income from the building on the site. In this case, the sale proceeds met the financing funds, so both the primary and the secondary lender were able to at least recover their principal investment and their accrued interest.

Both projects will be reconsidered in terms of uses and densities to increase their value, therefore amendments to the development permits and rezoning will have to be revisited. One of the projects previously had height limits because of view corridors but the view corridors on the site have since been removed, opening new opportunities to increase height and density.

The lesson from these case studies is that what appears to be solid and secure can change drastically when one or more variables change, such as an increase in interest rates or a downturn in the market. When the developer defaults on their loan repayment obligations, the land and associated assets need to be liquidated to repay the lenders. The bank (primary lender) and secondary lender need to find the highest value. But the sales offering is in a flat or declining market. This salvage operation is challenging, for the primary and secondary lender could have different objectives and are impatient to recover their investments. This situation can result in significant loss to one or all of the lenders, as witnessed in one of the case studies.

Choose partners carefully and share risks/rewards

As we can learn from the case studies just discussed, the real estate market follows up and down cycles. We need to plan for these cycles but at the same time be optimistic. Again, your partners are key in continuing to support the investment if the situation changes for the worse, otherwise the alternative is not desirable. That is why your partners, and especially the bank, want a solid covenant and verified assets as collateral before considering a loan. Choose your partners carefully.

In some cases, as mentioned previously, your partner could be another developer who has experience in developing mixed-use buildings, if you do not have that experience. The banker and investors will look for that experience to fund a loan. Alternatively, as discussed earlier, the vendor (landowner) could also be a partner. Instead of buying the property, which could be a substantial outlay of funds up front, you negotiate a partnership where, in return for the contribution, the vendor shares in the increased value of the property and associated profits.

You may need to exercise patience in choosing your partners. My wife and I have reviewed at least four builders already in Costa Rica. Your builder (general contractor) realizes your dream in real terms. They are core partners in executing paper plans. Connecting the architects and engineers with the contractor is crucial is attaining high performance throughout the construction phase, not just delivery of a product. Your buyers will immediately notice any *construction deficiencies*, namely, flaws that do not meet the predetermined standard (and must be rectified by the subcontractor, general contractor, or developer, depending on the conditions). On a related note, if *change orders*—being changes to the construction that were not considered in the construction drawings or budget—become commonplace, they could erode profits if they go beyond the allotted contingency in your development budget.

Figure 9. Partners can fill a specific gap
in the development team.

Defer cash investment and reduce risk

Be careful to manage the expectations of your investors and check the terms of their agreement. At the same time, ensure that "passive" partners (vendors) do not actively disrupt your business and the operation of the project. That is why a developer routinely buys the land with conditions, so the vendor does not unnecessarily get involved with the project and jeopardize the outcome. For example, the developer might set a condition that they make a down payment but that the rest of the required money is paid only when the municipality or district approves the rezoning for a new land use and increased density for the property. In setting this condition, the developer essentially decreases their risk and defers payments for one to two years or more.

Constantly refine ideas, drawings, and budget

Always remember that the development and design ideas will be refined throughout the design phases of the project. The market will change, and *pre-sales*—those 50 to 60% of sales required by the bank before construction financing is approved—are a determinant of success. The development idea evolves through design concepts, design development, schematic design, and construction drawings.

The same applies to the real estate development budget. The budget evolves from the earlier back-of-the-envelope analysis discussed in chapter 4—the rough calculation to help determine initial basic viability. This preliminary approach to financial projections evolves to a pro forma cash flow that includes detailed revenue sources, hard and soft costs, and profit measures. The pro forma itself evolves and changes to respond to changing variables like costs, revenue, and interest costs.

Constant refinement is the watchword, keeping in mind that quality control and cost controls are part of the filter and review system. As a real reminder that the project is not complete until the construction is done, here is a short anecdote. Moshe Safdie, the famous Canadian architect, and I were chatting in the newly completed National Gallery of Canada in Ottawa some years ago. "I didn't know if it would work," Safdie told me with a smile as he looked up and marvelled in the main rotunda entrance, the Scotiabank Great Hall. Above us was a spectacular glass and steel dome-like structure that created a wonderful spectacle of light on the ground surface below. His firm had designed it, but he didn't know until it was complete whether the structure and its quality of light would crystallize his intentions during the earlier design phase.

A caution regarding cost premiums with innovation

As I alluded to in chapter 1, be cautious regarding any project innovation that is not standard in its costing and details. As you move from idea to design development, the innovative ideas could create a significant cost premium if not grounded by experience and comparable projects, Cost control through estimating is important. For instance, the cost premium of Step 4 in the BC Energy Step Code is being implemented as the norm in construction. What does this mean to construction costs, and how will this squeeze the profit margins? Consumers will have to pay more, but how much more?

The same goes for other construction innovations, like passive house construction requirements, the recycling of water, or geothermal heating and cooling. Each of these will be associated with a cost premium. To quantify such costs, a prominent developer told me that a 5% premium can be absorbed in efficiencies over time, but a 10 to 15% premium eats into the project profit, without question. Stay mindful of the difference between "necessary" and "nice to have."

Value and valuations

I normally tell my teams that most next projects should be excellent and/or award-winning. Whatever you do, build value in every move so that if something goes wrong, you can sell the property for more than you purchased it for. Due diligence, master planning, rezoning, and the development permit should give confidence and more certainty to the next purchaser. If the documentation and narrative is comprehensive, well founded, and excellent, the value is normally higher.

Let's talk more about real estate value for a moment. Value of a real estate asset is perceived value in some respects, although quantified through real estate *appraisals*, carried out by a certified appraiser following industry norms. Canadian banks acknowledge appraisals as trustworthy. These appraisals normally compare similar properties and uses; they examine cash flow and the *capitalization rate*, namely, the expected return on investment, based on cash flow in rental or commercial leased properties. Special factors such as location, building age, construction method, quality, and property conditions either erode the estimated property value or elevate it.

However, in a hot market, a property value can be elevated and the property sell for well above the market valuation. Whereas in a depressed market, the property might receive no bids at all. Again, some of this valuation fluctuation is perceived value, not easily quantifiable because many forces are at play. Property value goes back to the fundamentals of supply and demand. In the case of low supply, demand normally increases along with value, and with high supply, the reverse happens.

When there are few properties (low supply and high demand) in an accelerating market affected also by decreasing interest rates, and a property has a premium location, there is upward price pressure on the property. The opposite happens—downward pressure on prices— when there are many properties on the market (high supply and low demand) and economic factors such as interest rates trending upward. Being the best in your market segment—in terms of quality, location, and price—normally creates the best-selling prices or lease rates. So, how do we define that competitive edge?

Competitive edge and understanding the buyer

Differentiating your housing, commercial, or industrial real estate product in the marketplace is important if not critical to success and creating a competitive edge, especially from an enduring valuation perspective. Do you want your product to be in demand and selling at optimum prices, or just another undifferentiated product in the marketplace?

The current market is a good test. We think we know the buyer. Think again. As one leading marketing executive shared, "We didn't really have to sell in the previous market with such elevated demand. Now we have to work to sell the product." Knowing what the buyer is looking for is a first step. To do that, you can use focus groups, consumer surveys, and thorough analysis of current data. Yes, and more if you can.

It is fascinating to observe where some development executives spend some or many of their weekends. They are not hanging out at posh resorts, but visiting real estate sales centres to see what the competition is doing and obtaining intelligence for their Monday morning project management meetings. Data can only tell you so much, as well as artificial intelligence obtained through tools such as chatbots. In-person experience and direct interviews still can help to make the difference.

Market analytics are taking a deep dive into not only past successes but also current consumer needs and projecting them forward. Various market and development data platforms provide local current market information. But what does it all mean? The basic package of granite countertops and quality appliances in kitchens and an open floor plan in the living area are not enough anymore. These elements are regarded as requirements in many cases. Now the next generation is beginning to define the desirable housing package in a particular location, depending on the projected demographic focus. Think flex rooms, quality not quantity of space, home offices, storage facilities, workshops, amenities, access to rapid transit, and unit variations.

Defining success

To define success as we strive for excellence, for starters we can use the basic business measurement of 12 to 18% return on cost or revenue as discussed and defined before (see chapter 4). This measurement can be used to compare the risks of other investments with that of a real estate investment (*opportunity cost*). In this case, compare return on investment with the return from a Guaranteed Investment Certificate (GIC).

If the return on investment is calculated at 6% for a real estate development, then a one-year GIC at 4.75% is almost comparable, and the development may therefore not be worth the risk. But say the real estate investment renders a projected 18% return on cost. Then it is worth pursuing, especially when the return could be eroded by unforeseen costs, an increase in borrowing costs, and extended approvals timing. Time is money.

Besides return on cost or revenue, the second element in defining success is the aspect of social and environmental benefits to the community. These elements and your corporate philosophy are important in gaining neighbour and community support and council approvals for the project.

Next-generation and long-term thinking involve climate change (some say "climate emergency"), green building, affordable housing contributions, and amenity contributions. Simply put, how can you positively contribute to the surrounding community, discussed earlier in the book as *net community gain*, without compromising the project or the basic return on investment? This can be a difficult question to answer, but I find that if you work with the community from the beginning to gain their trust, this approach normally also foregrounds reasonable and attainable community expectations.

Certainty and flexibility

With this elevated approach, real estate developers still need both certainty and flexibility. But isn't this a Catch-22? How can we expect both certainty and flexibility at the same time? On further examination, projects require certainty in land use and density but require flexibility to respond to changing markets and be able to adapt to a defined degree, including in their land use and density, to be successful.

In Garrison Crossing, Chilliwack, a Canada Lands Company development, our consulting group with the developer, Canada Lands Company (clc-sic.ca), strived to balance certainty and flexibility through the Comprehensive Development (CD) zone framework for the 60-hectare (150-acre) site. We created a minimum and maximum number of units on the property that limited density at reasonable levels and provided diversity in an area otherwise highly focused on single-family housing.[26]

Garrison Crossing was ahead of its time, allowing coach houses in a single-family neighbourhood in 2003. Our first market study suggested 25% multiple-family units and our second 35%. We found new niche markets, and the results exceeded expectations. In the end, Garrison Crossing has an estimated 75% multiple-family homes and 25% single-family homes (with 25% of the single-family homes having coach houses in the rear yards), foreshadowing the market trend visible today.

Techniques to elevate your practice

- Choose your partners carefully.

- Make sure that they are trustworthy and have the experience required.

- Keep your partners informed along the project timeline so they know early if there are issues and can help to resolve them.

- Continue to refine your approaches to align with market adjustments and construction requirements.

- Be careful with unnecessary innovation that costs more and decreases return on investment.

- Consider the future and current costs as you refine your development strategies.

- Each time you do a project, think of improving the product.

- Constantly improve and elevate throughout the project without compromising the return on investment or compromising your vision.

Key take-aways

Trusted partners are essential to a successful project. Investors, bankers, and contractors are your core partners. Once you have found an effective formula and the right team members, you can repeat your approach, but customize it to other projects. The first and some following projects will be the most challenging.

Refinement is a constant process since revenue and costs continually change. If sales revenue keeps increasing and costs are relatively constant, then profit normally increases. If sales revenue decreases and costs increase, the opposite happens. Adding or changing building materials, techniques, and/or technology adds costs and does not necessarily increase revenue, unless the consumer values the additions.

If you elevate your development process on a continual basis, your results should also improve. Through elevation, you excel and differentiate, rather than compete against another development project. The results of this approach will shine in three dimensions—economically, socially, and environmentally. And you will develop a richer and more robust community, rather than a lacklustre commodity.

The overriding message in this chapter is that you cannot develop real estate alone. You need the help of your partners and your real estate development team. With this additional support and extra lenses, you can build additional value in the property as you proceed.

In the next chapter, other community members will enter the picture that can influence your project. You may indeed consider a "third alternative" that satisfies not only your internal partners but also those in the community and the municipal or district councillors who ultimately approve your project. With a place-driven concept, a suitable site, thorough site review and testing, an elevated proposal, and the right team and partners (financing) in place, your project is now at the beginning of an approvals process that is largely out of your hands.

7

Approvals

Principle 7. Obtain a commitment or exit the approvals process.

> *Invent options for mutual gain. Focus on the people not the problem.*
> —Roger Fisher and William Ury

> *So, contrary to popular belief, people don't resist change—they resist being controlled.*
> —Ken Blanchard

To this point, you are still at the beginning of the development process. You have acquired the property or, in an even smarter strategy, will acquire the property on conditions or as part of a joint venture. The numerical analysis shows that the proposed project is viable from a return-on-investment perspective, but you have no formal approvals of the plans. The relationship-intensive part of the process in large part is just starting.

This chapter walks you through approvals and levels of risk depending on the status of the land, the approvals process, and the influencers who affect the final decision to proceed. This is the point where policy, politics, and process intersect in the development project.

Approvals and level of risk

There are three general levels of risk with approvals and the type of property, namely, raw rural or suburban land, zoned property, or zoned property with an income property. Let's take a look at all three.

- **Raw rural or suburban land.** This type of property carries the highest risk related to approvals, as the land probably has a rural or agricultural designation. If the property is in the Agricultural Land Reserve (ALR), the municipality must apply to the Provincial Agricultural Land Commission for its removal. In some cases, although the municipality has designated the property in its Official Community Plan and zoned it for urban use and density, no proposed development will be permitted unless the ALR underlying designation is removed. This process is complicated and removal from the ALR is highly unlikely in many cases. ALR lands are generally regarded as sacred and protected for agriculture by the Province of British Columbia.

  Rural lands are different and may be redesignated or zoned for higher-density housing or other uses, but within the urban growth boundary (e.g., Metro Vancouver, Fraser Valley Regional District), since these lands can be serviced with sanitary sewer and water. I have found that in areas outside Metro Vancouver, if the property is not close to urban services (water and sewer utilities), it may be years before you can obtain permissions for development. Creating your own utility to provide at least wastewater management is an option, but normally many housing units are required to create the economies of scale and therefore reduce costs, if your plan is considered for approval by the provincial health ministry. Otherwise, large lots with septic tanks and independent wells are the only alternative, if approved.

Municipalities and regional districts now prefer to build compact communities, so in a rural context you may be able to "cluster" development or, in other terms, transfer density from one part of the property to another to densify the development and even provide some compact housing, including townhouses, courtyard housing, duplexes, and triplexes.

If there is a possibility for redesignation (an Official Community Plan amendment) and rezoning (a change in land use and/or density), each of these processes takes considerable time (as much as 3 to 5 years) and can be combined for efficiency. I have been involved in processes that are continuing after ten years! These processes can be undermined on political grounds that have little to do with the merits of the proposal.

Rural land may be cheap, but what is the reason? Check with the municipality and review other similar applications, which are usually publicly available, to see where the challenges are and whether approvals are realistic. Approvals tend to follow a pattern, and if your application goes against the desirable land use patterns, approvals may be difficult (or impossible) and staff/community pushback significant. Be cautious and aware, investigate other approvals, and then decide whether to go ahead.

- **Zoned land.** Many developers who want to sell or build product quickly purchase property that is essentially "shovel ready." If the property is already zoned for the particular use and density, then the development permit and building permit are usually the subsequent approvals requirements. In other words, detailed construction drawings are required. Naturally, in zoned land situations, the price can be significantly higher, which can affect the viability of the project.

  In frequent cases, the vendor (original owner) of a suburban home or parcel tries to increase the land price to the point where the profit for redevelopment has been erased or is marginal. Sometimes these landowners will enter into a joint venture with the developer by contributing their land to the project in return for an ongoing interest in the capital appreciation and development proceeds, as mentioned earlier. The downside to this proposition is that developers would rather control the entire project than have joint venture partners getting involved that know little about development. With a silent partner, on the other hand, the arrangement could be perfect.

- **Zoned land with an income property.** A sweet spot for land acquisition is zoned land with an income property (e.g., an apartment building, retail or office space, or an industrial building) with secure tenants and substantial monthly income. This situation provides additional value and leverage for financing the redevelopment. It also provides a cash flow to the developer, investors, and the bank in case approvals are delayed, rezoning is required, or the project faces other construction delays. Zoned properties do have a downside if the revenue is from an apartment building, with mandatory payments to tenants on redevelopment to compensate for having to move out of the building.

This property will demand the highest price because of its inherent value, positive cash flow, and future redevelopment value if in a prime location near transit. Late in 2023, the Province of British Columbia passed legislation to advance higher densities, especially close to transit stations. The provincial government has also approved 3-, 4-, and 6-unit housing densities (near designated bus stops) on single-family lots, depending on location and lot size—a sweeping change that applies to all municipalities.[27]

Informal conversations do not mean approval

An informal conversation with a planner or economic development professional at the municipality or regional district, although helpful, does not assure formal approval of your project. Some developers used to say, "All we need is to rezone the property." But that statement oversimplifies the situation. The rezoning process is complicated and often unpredictable, and can be overwhelming in many instances.

As we have discussed, it is good to get all the facts, not only, with respect, an encouraging "sales pitch" from a realtor that does not tell the whole story and provide full background information. Not knowing enough is where risk lies. Hopefully, you have at least investigated the process, requirements, timeline, and possible pitfalls of a rezoning or other land use permissions from the municipality or regional district. Note that in B.C. this process can take up to three to five years and the outcome is uncertain, with politics part of the rigorous review and approvals process. Additional community amenity contributions are also uncertain in many cases, although they are becoming specific to the proposed land use and density rather than determined through a negotiated process.

No water and no sewer, no development

Some years ago, I was invited by a county near Calgary, Alberta, to make a presentation to the community and work on various development plans. I had been working throughout Alberta, including Calgary, for a few years. One senior staff member invited me into her office to show me the entire million acres that made up the county. I noticed that the map had small flags on various properties. I asked what the flags represented.

She responded by saying that these parcels had "development direction" from council. Now I became curious and somewhat alarmed. She then further explained that there had been proponent inquiries on the flagged properties and council had approved further investigations for potential development. Then I asked the fundamental servicing question: "Is there sewer and water available to these properties to allow development?" She said, "Not necessarily." I advised her to be very cautious providing "development direction," since this direction from council can be easily misinterpreted as potential approval possibilities or even official endorsement of a project, especially when presented to foreign or uninformed investors.

Remember that without water or sewer, you cannot get approval for development, except for large-lot development, if that. Infrastructure may be obvious and readily available in urban situations, but not so in more rural situations or properties on the urban edge. Even then, the water and/or sewer may have capacity challenges that need to be upgraded, in some cases at significant cost— referred to as *off-site costs*.

Pre-application to determine possibilities

Many municipalities have introduced a "pre-application" requirement before they formalize an application and request the associated fees. These application fees can be hefty, so a pre-application form, concept design, and meeting are good first steps to determine real feasibility and level of support from all internal departments at the municipality or regional district. Ensure you have consent from all landowners involved in a land assembly if you have not yet purchased their property.

These pre-applications are worth it to you as a developer, as they provide an opportunity to reconsider proceeding with the project before you have made too many financial commitments. They are likewise beneficial for the municipality or regional district, which does not want to commit to a project that has too many detractors and may be unrealistic in terms of feasibility and timely servicing as well as public and council support.

As you proceed with approvals, make sure you include all the steps and complete the content requirements. Confirm the process steps and timing as much as possible. It is often very difficult for the municipality or regional district to commit to a strict schedule, but obtain an estimate based on a completed internal and external circulation, review, and four required readings by council. For a more complete in-depth explanation of the formal approvals process, see *New Pathways to Approvals*.[28]

Heat chart and influencers

In real estate development approvals, the influential players are of critical importance. Whether it is the mayor, a councillor, the director of planning or engineering, the community association, or the local First Nations chief and council, all are valid "influencers," and one may have more influence than another.

I developed a useful heat chart that lists the influential parties in the development process and their extent of influence in the approvals process. For example, the municipal council or regional district board of directors each have the final say in approvals, so they are shown as having "high" influence in the process, while the planning advisory commission has a "medium" influence in the process. The commission may influence the final decision but does not make the final decision.[29]

The heat chart can be a project management tool to inform where energy and resources should be focused to build support for the project. It is good to carefully analyze your adversaries to understand their motivations. Only then can you possibly move them from project objector to project supporter by focusing on satisfying their specific concerns. As Abraham Lincoln was quoted as saying in a speech, "Do I not destroy my enemies when I make them my friends?"

This advice directly applies to participants and influencers in the approvals process, especially since the process is by nature political and this is the time when community influence comes onto the stage. Here are seven rules to keep in mind throughout your approvals process where public engagement rather than technical approvals is required:

1. **Keep staff informed.** Municipal or district staff should be aware of your public and council communication and engagement strategies. Staff are charged with the approvals process and council makes the final decision. Normally, council follows staff direction, but this presumed endorsement is not always the case. Be careful in navigating the approvals process with staff and council so that each knows what is going on. Division and misunderstanding can cause valuable time delays and erosion of support.

2. **Build community support.** From the beginning, engage with members of the community in informal settings, to build trust and understand their perspective. Develop a community support group that informs the rest of the community of progress and the status of the development as it proceeds. Ensure that the municipality or regional district is kept updated on your strategy and actions. Invite them also to your meetings so that they also know the concerns

of the community early in the process and can help explain to the community the municipal perspective and review process.

3. **Consult First Nations.** As part of the approvals process, you are required to consult with local First Nations. Actively engage with First Nations at the beginning of the approvals process. Hiring an Indigenous community consultant familiar with the First Nation and local protocols can support the exploration of world views, bridge perspectives, and create meaningful engagement.

4. **Develop separate community benefit packages.** These benefit packages are for the community and First Nations that respond to their individual wants and needs. This community benefit strategy could include potential on-site and off-site improvements (e.g., publicly accessible pathways, local park improvements, and street tree planting). In some cases, they may not be large expenditures, but these improvements will help in gaining support for your development proposal.

5. **Engage with the mayor and council.** Connect with the local mayor and council or regional board chair and council individually in an open and transparent way so that they can express their concerns and support. They are then aware of the application and any issues that you have addressed. These individuals have the final say in approvals, so late engagement is not acceptable, but continual engagement can be

a bridge to success and unanimous approval by council.

6. **Be prepared for the public hearing (if required).** Anything else besides objective unanimous support by council is a gamble, with a split-vote council (frequent structure) tending to err on the conservative side. In other words, a vote against approval is normal if the application is politically risky and the next election is within six months.

   In 2023, I was attending a public hearing as a member of the development team to provide a summary statement of the project's merits. The project was an excellent one, mixing environmental conservation with active public recreation. It offered a diversity of housing units, excluding single-family houses completely. Essentially, this project was a compact community incorporating significant environmental conservation and improvements.

   I was told that maybe 15 to 20 local residents would attend the public hearing and that approval of the project was almost a foregone conclusion, not even a close vote among members of council. Unfortunately, I was not actively leading the public engagement process, so it was impossible for me to predict the actual turnout at the event.

   To my utter surprise, more than 300 angry community members showed up at the public hearing. It was embarrassing for the development team and even degenerated into harassment and threats to council in the end. The situation was unfortunate, but I believe it could have been avoided by the developer actively engaging the community early, often, and effectively to gain trust and eventual endorsement. Instead, the final result was a vote of 6 to 1 against, with the mayor the only positive vote, as he did not intend to run again for office in the next election.

7. **Consider the third alternative.** As the project progresses in the approvals process, there is your proposal and the alternative proposed by the city or regional district. Be prepared to develop a third alternative together to bridge the gap. There are methods that bring common interests to the fore and separate the people from the problem, as explored in *Getting to Yes*, by Roger Fisher and William Ury, mentioned earlier, and *The Third Alternative*, by Stephen Covey.[30]

Many times, negotiating a third alternative is not easy as the different parties, including the Department of Fisheries and Oceans, Ministry of the Environment and Climate Change Strategy, and Ministry of Transportation and Infrastructure in British Columbia, to name a few, do not agree with each other. Finding a solution that is supportable is something that may take compromise or alteration of the project plan— hence the third alternative.

I have played the role of an arm's length facilitator or negotiator on large, complex projects that require someone without a vested interest in the project. Develop engagement rules, establish objective criteria for resolution, and set out to resolve the sticking points with all parties in the room. All aspects of the project need to be on the table, otherwise the negotiations can be undermined early or later.

Figure 10. Become an expert at approvals so the process is not a gamble but yields consistent results.

Review by council

The approvals process includes three readings by council and a final adoption of the bylaw (fourth reading) once staff approves or disapproves the development for council review. Sometimes, first reading is a symbolic meeting to allow a complete application to proceed, but this situation is changing as more information is being required up front, with more scrutiny by staff. The second reading, with external circulation to outside government agencies and a public hearing (if required), brings up more concerns and conditions for approval. Normally the third reading endorses the valid responses, and the fourth reading formalizes the legal aspects by spelling out the development agreement conditions between the municipality or regional district and the real estate developer.

The unexpected late hit

Be aware that anything can happen in between these reading stages, depending on the complexity of the project and its level of support. In one instance, the city manager of a municipality invited the developer to attend a one-on-one meeting prior to adoption of the development after an extensive review process. With the developer expecting a simple pleasant meeting going over some of the details, instead the city manager introduced an ultimatum—either the developer reduced their developable land from 33% to 25% or the municipality would defer approval of the application. When the developer politely asked the city manager the reason behind the sudden change, he simply said, "I promised it to someone."

There was no prior warning of this change to the development plan, and this deferral of the application could delay the project's approval by another six months or more. Obviously there was not earned trust between the city administration and this development group, resulting in an unfortunate result after such a long approvals process and countless complex amendments to the plan. The developer had no choice and had to approve the change, without adequate discussion and rationale.

Techniques to elevate your practice

- Know the approvals process that applies to your development project.

- Translate the given process to your template and have it approved by the approval authority.

- Build support with all "influencers" from the beginning, including First Nations and the community.

- Consider retaining an Indigenous public engagement consultant to ensure that First Nations engagement is culturally sensitive and effective.

- Engage individually with the mayor and members of council in an open and transparent way so that they can express their concerns and support.

- Develop, if necessary, the third alternative together with the municipality or regional district.

- Anticipate the public hearing if required (Official Community Plan amendment).

- Be prepared for changes.

- Count your votes on council—those for and those against. Make sure your application is significantly supported, otherwise the final approvals are a gamble not worth taking.

Key take-aways

Approval of a development proposal is not simply a technical checklist anymore, unless it is beyond the requirement of a rezoning. Even then approval can be complicated, demanding, and time-consuming. Be sympathetic to and work with the municipality or regional district. They have their own job to do and their specific requirements. Be respectful. Gaining ultimate approval is a complex process that takes time and energy. Be aware of the "influencers" and work with staff, the community, First Nations, and council to build unanimous support for your project.

Finally, you are at the end of the approvals process. No, you are not. You still must gain approvals in constructing the building(s) and completing the site improvements. You will need construction inspections and occupancy permits based on meeting the BC Building Code and other regulations governing real estate development.

The next chapter digs into the pre-planning of construction, construction itself, and occupancy, while keeping your investors, contractors, and buyers happy with the progress, quality, and timeliness of completion. Not an easy task, but let's now explore what the ingredients of a successful construction process and product look like.

8

Construction

Principle 8. Follow your design with the right trusted team.

Invest in detail early in the pre-construction process.
—Executive vice-president

This chapter describes how you build your dream development. To this point in the development process, nothing has been built on your site, except potential development application signage. Development has been a theoretical exercise. Now is the time when theory meets construction. This phase includes pre-construction planning, working drawings, tendering, construction, occupancy, and customer care. Holding onto your vision, while maintaining flexibility in a disruptive market and an arena of inflating costs, is a dance that strikes a balance between dreams and realistic implementation. Altogether it's not an easy path, with the push of getting things done and also doing them well in unpredictable times. Let's assume we take a positive attitude—endure and stay the course.

Remember that having a commitment to excellence is important but the pragmatics of the real world will erode ideals at least a bit—or a great deal. Subtle adjustments are important to attain the goal. I remind myself of the age-old saying "When the going gets tough, the tough get going." Taking action even in difficult situations is key. I say to my teams: "I get paid for four minutes a day to make tough decisions and to close the deals." So, keep these credos in mind as you implement your development plans.

Construction pre-planning process and budgets

First, let's look at the construction process as both an on-site and an off-site process. You must love to get your feet and hands dirty. This is the gritty nexus of construction where contractors, subcontractors, materials, weather, and site intersect.

Construction overall comprises a standard set of steps that are, in part, parallel tracked, from a project management perspective. In other words, the degree to which each stage is activated depends on the completion of other tasks. For example, the marketing illustrations are not started until the working drawings are 70 to 80% complete. The working drawings (more on them below) are continually being refined until they are fully approved at the final building permit stage. And the final working drawings (referred to as 100% drawings) are issued for final construction.

This pre-planning phase determines the rest of the project to a large degree. Time is well spent in refining scheduling, design, materials, costing, the right contractor and subcontractor team, marketing strategies (for pre-sales and sales), revenue forecasts, and contingency planning. Construction staging is also important to set up the site and adjoining properties properly, including the length of crane swings, foundation impacts, access points, materials storage, daily hours, and safety precautions.

As we saw in chapter 4, the budgeting process ranges from a Class D budget, which is preliminary and highly variable, to a Class A budget that is based on 100% working drawings. Again, here are how cost estimates over time relate to evolution of working drawings:

- *Class D costs*—acquisition and preliminary schematic conceptual design
- *Class C costs*—development permit stage (design development), with 30 to 60% working drawings
- *Class B costs*—building permit stage, with 60 to 70% working drawings
- *Class A costs*—tendering for construction and detailed design complete, with 100% working drawings

Development permit, building permit, and working drawings

Although not considered part of the direct construction process, preparing development permit drawings influences the final design by moving from *schematic design* to *design development*. Schematic design is preliminary design and is not as detailed as design development. Schematic design is for preliminary concept discussions, while design development is used for the formal development application. Design development ensures that the project is feasible to be built and includes more details. Costs evolve from a Class D level to a Class C level, as discussed earlier.

Municipalities are requiring more and more detail at this relatively early design stage. Yet developers should be cautious not to specify too much at this stage, since further detailed design work is required. Sometimes developers combine a rezoning (change of land use and/or density) and development permit submission to save time. This approach requires more details earlier in the process.

For example, the efficiency of the building is monitored closely even at the development permit stage. *Building efficiency* means the difference between the total gross square footage and the saleable area. To illustrate, when the building efficiency is only 75%, then 25% of the building is in the form of common area or elevators and hence not paid for by sales or rents. In comparison, when the efficiency is 83%, then only 17% is paid for by the other 83% of saleable or rentable area. In this case, you gain 8% saleable or rentable areas, as compared to the earlier design. As you can see, the efficiency of the building can significantly affect the potential revenue from sales or rents and associated profit for the project.

In development approvals, the development permit progresses to the building permit as the next step in the process. The general level of detail required, as just discussed in the working drawing stage, increases significantly. The required list of drawings is extensive and comprehensive. Building code requirements are reviewed in detail to ensure they are met. These building permit drawings become the "drawings of record" for the municipal building inspectors when they inspect your site. Conformance with these drawings is not an option but a requirement. Any deviation from the drawings as approved requires an amendment, which can be time-consuming. The lesson here is to get everything right the first time.

The term *working drawings* refers to the precise scale drawings required by professionals such as the architect, landscape architect, structural engineer, electrical engineer, civil engineer, and others. The list of professionals and associated details is expanding as development requirements expand. For instance, the progression from Step 3 to Step 4 in the BC Energy Step Code demands further details.

Working drawings comprise a number of specific drawings and specifications (materials, applications, and requirements) that together define the construction requirements. It is important that these drawings be reviewed by a qualified professional (e.g., registered architect, engineers, and landscape architect) so they all work together and do not feature any significant conflicts. The mechanical systems can be an area where issues arise, since the electrical, plumbing, sprinkler, and heating systems must be coordinated, aligned to service multiple units, and connected to off-site sources.

To summarize, the following list shows the degree of completion of working drawings and the classification of costing at different stages of construction:

- *Development permit*—30 to 60% working drawings (Class C costs)

- *Building permit*—60 to 70% working drawings (Class B costs); 70 to 80% working drawings required to start marketing illustrations

- *Tender*—90% working drawings (Class B to Class A costs)
- *Issued for construction*—100% working drawings (Class A costs)

The *tendering* of the project is usually undertaken with working drawings that are 90% complete. Tendering is the process in which the project invites qualified general contractors to submit bids to construct the project along with subcontractors. The tendering process is complex, since it involves the development of complete pricing and terms that should include enough flexibility to modify prices if required due to a change in scope, normally through what is referred to as a change order.

Trust and an established track record are crucial in determining a winning bid. In most cases, a combination of price, comprehensiveness, and established reputation wins the project bid. The general contractor with the winning bid works closely with the development manager and coordinators to confirm the construction schedule, budget, and overall contractual arrangements.

The contracts can vary from standard contracts to include the following:

- CCDC 2 – 2020—*stipulated price* contract (upset price)
- CCDC 3 – 2016—*cost-plus* contract that has a specific cost with additions
- CCDC 5A – 2010—*construction management* contract for *services*

- CCDC 5B – 2010—*construction management* contract for *services and construction*
- CCDC 14 – 2013—*design-build stipulated price* contract (upset price)

Figure 11. Construction is a trusted partnership between multiple parties who strive for constant improvement.

Marketing and launch

Marketing ideas ideally start at the beginning of the project as the project idea, vision, goals, targets, and strategies start to develop, as discussed in chapter 1. Questions such as the following demand detailed answers: What is the target market and what are their spatial requirements? At what price? With what amenity requirements? Each of these questions is a critical area of inquiry right from the beginning, and the answers help to shape the project design.

The project marketing illustrations start to take shape during the building permit stage and are refined for the sales centre on the site or elsewhere prior to construction. Pre-sales can begin following development permit approval, since the primary lender now requires up to 60% pre-sales prior to funding construction. The development and building permits as well as pre-sales define the parameters for construction financing. Marketing professionals should take an active role in reviewing the design drawings to ensure that all of the subtle buyer requirements are included.

Construction and safety

Construction starts when work begins on the site, whether it be for staging construction access, materials, and storage to erecting hoarding and taking safety precautions around the entire site. Safety is a constant and an important element of supervising events, utilizing foresight to avoid unsafe conditions.

Several permits are required before you start any disturbance on the site, including demolition and excavation permits, tree removal permits (where applicable), and others that may apply. Ensure that all permits are issued, otherwise a stop-work order can halt all momentum and delay construction. Be sure to communicate with the neighbours in advance regarding schedules, so they are aware before any site disturbance occurs.

Be careful during this initial part of the process, for the demolition often creates a significant change in the neighbourhood or area. Neighbourhood trust and support can be shattered easily with one significant tree being removed without a permit or, worse, on municipal property. Make sure barriers are erected that protect the retained trees and that these trees and their root systems are not damaged.

Excavation is another sensitive area that can affect neighbours with sound and proximity to their property. Additionally, excavators need to be sensitive to archaeological finds. Should Indigenous remains or artifacts be suspected or discovered, be sure to follow appropriate protocols.[31] The importance of investigating archaeological sites cannot be overstated. Recently a developer in the City of Vancouver sold a property after discovering First Nations artifacts, when the future of the site and construction timing and costs became uncertain.

Building construction and landscape

The foundation of a building creates the frame for the building. If it is wrong, the whole building suffers. There is zero tolerance for error. If the foundation is not exact in its dimensions or geometry, the subsequent floors and walls will be incorrect. Monitoring and inspecting construction as it progresses is critical to success.

Landscape construction (hardscape concrete forms, walls, as well as associated electrical conduits and plumbing) needs to be executed in tandem with building construction in many cases. The soft landscape can be completed later to avoid unnecessary damage but needs to be in place, in conformance with the landscape drawings, for the building to pass final inspection and gain occupancy permits.

The timing and overlap of construction contractors and materials delivery are essential to meet projected deadlines and budgets. Weekly meetings on site are critical to bring the construction and development team together, build trust, resolve issues early, and discuss next steps. Walk the site, discuss the issue, and use team problem-solving to resolve any issues, thereby creating a shared can-do approach.

When circumstances change and the developer wants items added or deleted, this situation requires a change order that also necessitates first agreement and then signatures from the contractor and the developer. This change order then affects the budget, materials, and construction. Normally, change orders are accounted for in the 5% contingency built into or as specified within the project budget. The change order could be an exchange of a bathtub for a shower. But even this change could affect many if not all apartment units and the building permit drawings (plumbing, fixtures, and floor plans). Not an easy fix. Carefully evaluate each change order to ensure it is essential and required—or explore an alternative.

Site inspections by the development project team, the contractor, or subcontractor supervisors are essential to ongoing success on the construction site. In addition, regular inspections by the municipal inspector are required as construction progresses. In the City of Vancouver, areas have assigned inspectors. Build a relationship with your inspector early and be forthright, when possible, to resolve issues early, otherwise small issues can grow into big issues quickly and unnecessarily.

With an established, trusted relationship with your inspector, final inspections will be easier. Anticipate unresolved project issues with permit approvals. Develop a mutually supported method of timely resolution to meet the occupancy timeline.

Post-construction occupancy and customer care

When your tenant or owner takes occupancy, the work is not over. There is a warranty period in which construction deficiencies will be noted. A prompt response to these deficiencies, with quality cleanup or replacement of materials or fixtures, is important to gain client support and positive reviews. In the longer term, these clients could age in place or move to your next project. You want to keep them happy and manage reasonable requests in a timely and professional manner.

Improving construction processes and results

Let's examine more closely two aspects of construction. The first is the inclusive concept of "best idea wins." The second is constant improvement and refinement of the drawings.

- **Best construction idea wins.** It is interesting to observe inflexibility in conversations and intentions. When you are working with a development team, it is always good to listen with two ears and speak with one mouth. In other words, to speak half as much as you listen. To understand first and then be understood always fuels a more informed and respectful conversation, otherwise unnecessary anger and frustration can dominate.

  A "listen first" approach is smart and works well, especially in an informed and competitive conversation or meeting. Include everyone, exclude no one. This practice results in the communal development of the best idea with, in most instances, broad support. Otherwise, you may control the conversation or meeting but gain little support and get few meaningful contributions to the project or idea. You lost by your ego taking over.

Be attuned to your manner of communication as you construct your plan. Investors, bankers, development team members, community members, councillors, and municipal staff or regional district staff will question the merits of the ideas, plans, and related details you put forward. Be ready to respond by using an *active listening* approach to respond constructively. You are listening first to what the person is saying and meaning. After listening to understand, you respect the person by asking more questions or commenting on their discussion points.

You are learning in the process, rather than speaking about something you already know. In some instances, at the city manager level, you really have no choice but to listen. In other situations, these two-way conversations could result in small changes with bigger results. That is why we say the "best idea wins."

- **Refinement is a constant process.** You are always searching for a better or more refined solution, making continual adjustments to your processes and plans. It is like trimming your sails on open water to achieve the optimum speed. Your job is never done until you give the owner or renter the key to their home, office, industrial warehouse, or some other unit. Even then, there is learning and recording for your next project or providing customer care over the next year. Remember that this customer could be a customer for life!

I have questioned municipalities and developers about the importance of monitoring and evaluation in learning for the next project. One municipality had spent $150,000 to monitor and evaluate a new stormwater management system, including curbside rain gardens, and concluded that monitoring was too expensive.

Some developers might dismiss monitoring and evaluation as costly, time-consuming, and of limited value. Staff at ETRO Construction of Burnaby, B.C., a construction management and general contracting firm, think otherwise. They are constantly reviewing their construction projects to better understand where they can save time, save money, and improve quality throughout their projects.

Techniques to elevate your practice

- Pre-plan construction, with special attention to staging and budgets.
- Hire a winning and trusted construction team.
- Refine the construction drawings and costs and start to execute the project.
- Remember that improvement and refinement of drawings is a continuous process.
- Know that trust and an established track record are crucial in determining a winning contractor bid to construct the project.
- Implement "best idea wins" to resolve construction issues, the idea that is most cost-efficient and has the most benefits.
- Inspect your site throughout construction, mindful of "safety first."
- Support your tenants and buyers after the project is complete.
- Listen to learn from others and continually upgrade your processes.
- Monitor and evaluate your construction process for constant improvement.

Key take-aways

Build the best project, balancing budget with quality, but be open to change with an active listening approach where the "best idea wins," always increasing value and reducing risks where possible. Refinement is a constant process.

We have come to the end of the development process but we are really at the beginning of learning from experience and wisdom. We started by examining the essence of real estate development and the fundamental elements of the process, from idea to execution. In turn, we reviewed important influences and future thinking, the place-driven idea, market and finance factors, site review and testing, partners and elevation, approvals, and construction. I hope you have become aware of the complexities of the changing and evolving development process and what is required to strive for success in every project. There is also the higher calling that is paramount—to build great communities for our growing and aging population. So, we aren't quite finished yet.

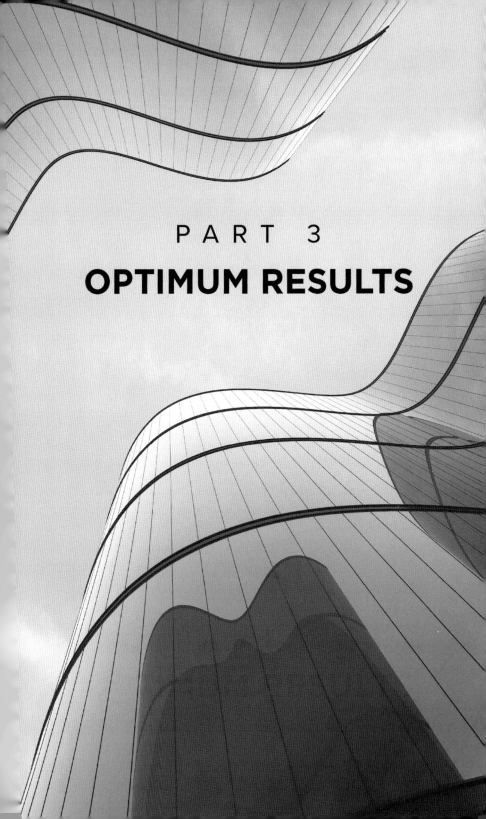

PART 3
OPTIMUM RESULTS

9

Higher Returns

Principle 9. Focus on your strengths and give back.

> *To improve is to change; to be perfect is to change often.*
> —Winston Churchill

> *Far better is it to dare mighty things, to win glorious triumphs, even though checkered by failure . . . than to rank with those poor spirits who neither enjoy nor suffer much, because they live in a gray twilight that knows not victory nor defeat.*
> —Theodore Roosevelt

I have reserved this final chapter to discuss the fundamental aspect of making challenging choices that are team or community based, informed by policy and new ideas. I finish with twelve pearls of wisdom that I hope will inspire you to action—somewhere in the real estate industry. If you are already a development professional, I hope you have gained some insights from this book that have enriched your understanding or simply given you further confidence in what you do. Now, as to decision-making in property development, here are my main pointers.

Give people choices

When you are presenting a proposal to key decision-makers, it is beneficial and strategic to provide people with choices. That way they can make their own decisions based on assumptions and analysis. To do otherwise is to put both the decision-makers and your team in a precarious position. When yes or no are the only choices, you have a 50% chance of losing. And if there is risk involved, your decision-makers will probably decide against the proposal. Not a promising prospect.

However, if you present three choices—optimistic, realistic, and pessimistic—decision-makers can see the merits and detractions of each. Then they make a more informed decision. They can also approve the project moving forward with conditions, changes in details, or a variation of one option. This approach can address the concerns, especially about future projections, of a conservative cynic (banker or investor) who may favour the pessimistic approach, which essentially could condemn every development. Hopefully, with some luck, balance, realism, and general support will win the day after discussion and refinement of one of the options presented, which may combine realistic and optimistic forecasts.

Walk the site: Boots-on-the-ground due diligence before optimism

If you are presented with a project that has a tone of over-optimism, be cautious, for someone is trying to sell you something versus present the project in an objective way. I recall clearly the time I was called into a development company a few years ago to help guide and shape their future. The company was working on several potential development sites throughout the Vancouver region. I always like walking a site and discovering for myself the constraints to development.

One of the company's potential sites was in a rural area east of Vancouver, in the Fraser Valley. I was excited about the site as it had frontage on the Fraser River, but cautious nonetheless. The company's executive vice-president and I visited the site on a picturesque summer day. The weather was perfect and the scenery outstanding as we drove through the valley. We parked at the edge of the approximately 10-hectare (25-acre) site and walked into the central area, which was open and vacant. A few manufactured homes dotted the site on the western edge. Immediately, significant required setbacks along the Fraser River came into play and reduced the potential development footprint. One red flag.

At first, I envisioned a wonderful resort of cabins with an active waterfront. Then the dominant red flag appeared as I entered a mature forest in the western section of the site. I stopped in my tracks. Before me were what were described to me as more than ten First Nations burial mounds that apparently dated, as I found out soon after, back at least three hundred years. Each of these extensive mounds was up to 2 metres in height and 5 metres long (6½ feet high and 16½ feet long). Fir trees a century old or more were growing out of some of the mounds, suggesting that they were very old.

No development could ever happen here, for this was sacred First Nations ground. Eventually, on our return from our site inspection and after further discussions, the development company astutely withdrew from the potential joint venture.

Choose the right location

Sometimes, as developers, we get overly excited about a property's development prospects because of the land's price. We tend to overlook the fundamentals that determine that lower price. It is not a lower price for nothing; there are reasons the price is appealing and below market. In other instances, the property appears to have an attractive location and has some potential for development. Have other professionals investigate the property to ensure there are no "deal-breakers" or substantial issues.

Back in 2006, a client wanted to develop the wrong piece of land in Vladivostok, Russia. This was well before the president of the Russian Republic, Vladimir Putin, decided to invade the Crimea. My senior engineer and myself were introduced to this Russian real estate developer through Canada Mortgage and Housing Corporation. We were to review the land and develop a master plan for it. We walked the site, talked to local officials, and then it struck me on the third day that our client had the wrong land. The property was a former air cadet military base (so probably contaminated), was located on a river delta (so low in elevation, with unstable soils), and was situated at the end of a bay on the Pacific Ocean (so susceptible to a potential tsunami). When we met with our client, he appreciated our honesty and critical analysis.

We suggested that his company buy the higher ground above. Its stable soils, better access, and improved views made the property superior to the lower ground, which could still be used for recreation. We developed a master development plan for housing overlooking the bay, in line with the less risky scenario. One of the problems with our proposal was that a sizable portion of the upper land was owned by a senior naval official of the Russian Pacific Fleet, and our client said it would take a US$4000 lunch in Moscow to even start the acquisition conversation.

Pay attention to policy interpretation

In my experience, often not enough time and scrutiny are devoted to the current policy that determines the land use and extent of development on a land parcel, especially in suburban and rural areas with the most potential for development. Sit down with the planner and ensure that you are "interpreting" correctly what is written down. Find out what the current and emerging unwritten, but supportable, policies are to direct your future-oriented proposal. Verify your interpretation of policy with the director of development and/or director of planning to ensure it is consistent with actual policy and can be used in the project application submission.

In urban areas, the policy directions tend to be more straightforward and direct. But I need to temper that statement too, for I just reviewed a proposal in downtown Vancouver that involved delayed heritage revitalization. The proposal had excellent merit but ran into issues around heritage bonuses and policy interpretation.

Again, keep in mind that rural land development and accompanying policies are in place to protect the rural character and limit development outside designated growth areas—normally towns and villages. With that understanding, let's look at another case study that did not proceed—at least so far. This property again is in the Fraser Valley, in the far eastern section governed by the Fraser Valley Regional District. In this case, all the engineering and environmental preliminary analysis of the site development proposal had been completed. I was called in to briefly look at the findings and help determine the development potential and limitations. This potential client had done the engineering and environmental analysis but did not factor in planning policy in the feasibility study.

It can be daunting to review and interpret all the current land use policies, but doing so is worth the time and energy. In this case, I found the policies included significant environmental flooding, water control, and access issues. When combined with the restrictive and limited development potential policies, these posed significant impediments to any development application. The policies clearly expressed that the regional district wanted to limit development in the area and had the physical, environmental, and access issues to support its position. This finding was unfortunate, but clear after a review of policy and the reason I changed my initial reaction regarding the site from optimistic to conservative, with limited development potential, if any.

Balance new approaches with tested applications

On the one hand, in development we have the status quo, which in some instances produces the "same old product" without improvements. This product is feasible since it has already been built and proven to be successful. Form follows financial success. Bankers and investors are trying to protect their investment, and any undue risk will affect their views of a project.

On the other hand, we have innovative ideas in building technology, emerging building materials, and carbon-neutral policy directions. Be careful to balance project changes with feasible processes and products. You want to have a competitive edge, but at what cost? I am conservative by nature, so if a new product has been tested, been approved, and the builder is trained in its application at a near-equivalent price, I am supportive. Otherwise, I would stay with the current application to match building code requirements and proceed with little risk.

Find your place in the spectrum of development

A career in real estate development, like life, is a process and can be enjoyed each step of the way. My father, as an architectural engineer, told me once that he didn't work a day in his life since he enjoyed what he did so much. He also coached me to find a career where if it becomes "work," find another job. I also love what I do, which is a combination of consulting, financing, teaching, coaching, and writing. Of course, the same can be said for real estate development as for anything else, that there will be some (hopefully minor) more grinding part of the job that makes you enjoy the other parts more.

What parts of real estate development flow naturally and are enjoyable? Discover these for yourself. Stephen Covey said, "Start with the end in mind."[32] Once you know your goal, create a series of steps and a vision. This is what I call your treasure map. In my experience, if you plot out what you want to happen physically—on a map, in a diagram, or in words—you will reach your destination for it is embedded in your subconscious, which helps to direct your behaviours towards your goal. Hence, you will find the treasures you are seeking.

Property development is a multi-dimensional business with many parts, from the front end to the back end of the process. These parts include idea development, property acquisition, finance, planning, design, quantitative analysis, approvals, marketing, accounting, project management, and construction management. Part of the challenge is to find where you fit best.

First, get into the game and learn the rules. For those already engaged in development, up your game through experience and the accrued wisdom that comes from it. Sometimes, a development company is too big to give you a feel for the whole process, and you can become typecast in a certain role—say, marketing—that you are good at but with which you become bored over time. Aspiring to a project management position will get you broad experience in many if not all the facets of real estate development.

In a smaller company, you may have the chance to work on small projects that are not as complex but give you the hands-on experience you need to work on the larger projects, as you evolve and mature. Earn your promotions and learn from the more experienced developers, since they have already made the mistakes that they remember and don't repeat.

Many of the trending business books discuss learning from one's mistakes. I don't want you to dwell on mistakes, but do remember them as you strive for consistent success. I have worked in development management and project management, finance, design, and planning. I was also brought up in a construction family, so I have been fortunate to have acquired lived experience in many aspects of development. I have found my preferred home in development planning, design, and approvals. Finding opportunities was not always easy, but when one door closed, another one opened. Appreciate every step with gratitude and a positive attitude as you go through the next open doorway.

Twelve pearls of wisdom

I conclude this book with twelve pearls of wisdom, gathered from my decades in the business, to either inspire your journey into real estate development or refine your practice. Use these pearls as a call to action and to help guide you on your pathway to success.

1. Follow your calling, love what your do, and strive to deliver something bigger than yourself.
2. Look at the big picture and the small picture to ensure you are not acting in a vacuum.
3. Inspire yourself by thinking ahead for the next generation.
4. Develop value where no one else sees it or adopt a great idea.
5. Use quantitative analysis as a measurement tool and set success targets that are well founded and grounded.
6. Pay it forward and get twice the returns.
7. Include all stakeholders in the approvals process, or you can get blindsided.
8. Actively listen and learn to find wisdom that is timeless.

9. Be inspired by your heart, listen to your head, and trust your gut to reconsider.

10. Find enduring satisfaction and fulfillment in doing things that create broader community gain.

11. Gain clients for life through your commitment to quality, integrity, and accountability.

12. Leave a legacy that makes the world a better place and keeps on giving.

Figure 12. I offer twelve "pearls of wisdom" to help inspire your successful future in real estate development.

ACKNOWLEDGEMENTS

As always, I am grateful for my wonderful partners in real estate development—teaching colleagues, business associates, friends, and members of my book production team—who are unfailingly supportive. In particular, I sincerely thank the Urban Development Institute, Pacific Region, for their continued support and partnership in helping to train the next generation of developers in a way that is environmentally sensitive, socially responsible, and economically viable. Specifically, thanks to Verna Yu, director of professional development and programming; Anne McMullin, president and chief executive officer; and Jeff Fisher, vice-president and senior policy advisor. Together, we are always trying to improve our game at the FortisBC School of Development.

The School of Development continues to inspire my mission to help teach and coach professionals across the province of British Columbia. Its popularity and success continue after more than twenty years. This book is intended to become a resource for The Fundamentals of Real Estate Development, the school's introductory course. For the first time last year, we have developed a fourth course, Digging into the Dirt Behind Construction, which also informed these writings.

My professional development, planning, and teaching colleagues provided valuable stories, information, and insights that have brought this book to life. My special colleagues Mike Harcourt, Andy Yan, David Witty, Mark Holland, Bob Scragg, Michael Nygren, and Charlotte Connor deserve special note. Other important people include Briana Mussatto, Jessica Tempesta, Joe Varing, Jason Metcalfe, Mark Ankenman, Emily Kearns, Sandra Lee,

Cal Srigley, Scott Romses, and Paul Turje, who have all directly or indirectly added content to this book.

My wife Laura and daughter Athena have listened to countless ideas and balanced the presentation and content. Athena especially provided additional insights as a real estate development professional herself. I am so proud of her accomplishments and commitment.

Finally, my book production team members have been awesome. Naomi Pauls, my editor, has been brilliant with her eagle eye for not only content and associated logic but collective messaging in the whole package. Betty Chiu did an excellent job in refining the book's graphics and adding magic to the front cover. Finally, Tellwell assembled the whole package and ensured that the final book meets or exceeds professional standards.

To one and all, a heartfelt thank-you for a job well done!

GLOSSARY

amenity cost charges (ACCs). A new development finance tool that allows local governments to collect funds for amenities like community centres, recreation centres, daycares, and libraries from new development that results in increased population. These amenities support livable and complete communities in areas of growth.

appraisals. Property assessments completed by a certified appraiser for a financial institution following industry norms, to ascertain the worth of a property based on highest and best use.

area structure plan. A formal land use planning document in Alberta that lays out the types of land uses proposed for an area and addresses matters such as density, water supply, sewage disposal, stormwater drainage, environmental issues, and fire suppression.

back-of-the-envelope analysis. A one-year basic profit projection (revenue minus costs), used to determine a viable purchase price from a preliminary perspective.

building efficiency. The saleable area of a building (not including elevators or common areas) as a percentage of the building's total gross square footage.

capital stack. The organization of all capital contributed to finance a real estate transaction, defining who has the rights (and in what order) to the income and profits generated by the property throughout the hold period and upon sale.

capitalization rate. Expected *return on investment*, based on estimated net operating income. The capitalization (cap) rate simply represents the yield of a property over a one-year time horizon, assuming the property is purchased on cash and not on loan.

change orders. Changes to the construction that were not considered in the construction drawings or budget, which add to the budget and are formally approved by the developer.

circular economy. As in nature, everything is treated as a resource and is recycled, generating little or no waste.

coach house. An auxiliary dwelling unit located in the rear yard with parking below and a single living unit above.

community. Normally a collection of residential land uses and support facilities like commercial uses, schools, and emergency services that have a unique identity. Sometimes a community is made up of a number of smaller neighbourhoods.

community amenity contributions (CACs). Fees, whether in-kind or cash contributions, collected by a municipality when it grants development rights through rezoning.

community benefit strategy. A collection of community benefits that may include social and physical benefits (e.g., community interior and exterior space at no or reduced cost).

construction deficiencies. Flaws in construction that do not meet the predetermined standard and are normally rectified by the subcontractor, general contractor, or developer, depending on the conditions.

context sensitivity. In site planning, taking into account the surrounding land uses, roads, services, and environmental elements (e.g., forests, streams, orientation, and views) and considering them as part of the site design.

covenant. A developer's experience and trusted, successful track record of executing projects on time and on budget.

design development. Design work used for a formal development application, more detailed than *schematic design*, to ensure the project is feasible to be built.

development cost charges (DCCs). Fees collected from developers by a municipality or regional district to offset their infrastructure expenditures in servicing a new development, including water, sewer, drainage, and roads as well as fire protection facilities (e.g., fire halls), police facilities, and solid waste facilities. They also include cost-shared provincial highway projects, like interchanges and highway exits. Municipalities will be able to collect and use DCCs to finance their portion of highway facilities that are cost-shared between the province and the municipality.

eco-industrial network (EIN). A systems approach with lessons from nature minimizing waste and maximizing partnerships in value-added products. In practice, EIN creates collaborative relationships (networks) between businesses, governments, and communities to more efficiently and effectively use resources, such as materials and energy, but also including land, infrastructure, and people.

floor space ratio (FSR) or floor area ratio (FAR). The gross floor area of a building divided by the gross site area. FSR or FAR is the ratio of the building to the lot area. For example, if the building areas cover 100% of the site with one floor, that equals 1.0 FSR or FAR. Alternatively, if the building area covers half the site with two floors, it is still 1.0 FSR or FAR.

full-cost accounting. Monetizing the environmental and social impacts on a community in addition to the fiscal returns on the project.

genius loci. "Spirit of place," a concept used by the Romans and today used in urban design. It is a holistic approach—including psychic, physical, and human components of a physical space—in other words, the intangible quality of a material place, perceived both physically and spiritually.

hard costs. Costs to improve a development site that are directly related to construction (e.g., materials and labour, landscaping).

high-rise apartments. Buildings with more than twelve storeys.

internal rate of return (IRR). Calculation of the rate at which the *net present value (NPV)* of an investment equals zero, expressed as a percentage (rate of return).

leverage (vb). Reduce cash input to increase your *return on investment* by the use of other funding sources.

loan to value ratio (LVR). Total loan compared to the current appraised value of the property.

mid-level or mid-rise apartments. Buildings that range from seven to twelve storeys.

missing middle. The range of housing types between single-family housing and high-rise apartments, typically including townhouses, duplexes, triplexes, four-plexes, three- to six-storey apartments, and mid-rise apartments. Also called middle densities.

mixed-use development. Developments that include a variety of uses, from commercial to residential. In a standard situation, a mixed-use developments has commercial uses (e.g., retail shops) on the ground floor with residential uses above.

multiple-family residential. Attached residential development that includes duplexes, triplexes, four-plexes, townhouses, and apartments. This housing type is distinctive from single-family development in that single-family homes are detached (separate) houses.

negative leverage. A financing situation where the present return from an asset is lower than the interest rate of the mortgage.

net community / environmental gain. A positive improvement in the environmental, economic, and social well-being in the community.

net present value (NPV). Calculation of the difference between what an investment costs over years of development phasing and its present value, which helps determine whether the return will be worthwhile.

off-site costs. Expenses related to construction that are spent outside the actual site (e.g., costs for extending roads, sewers, and water lines to the site).

opportunity cost. A measure that compares other investments to real estate and what other opportunities would yield in financial and other non-quantifiable terms, like social and environmental ramifications.

passive housing. Homes designed to have the most energy-efficient building envelope. They require less energy to heat and cool and significantly reduce greenhouse gases.

pedestrian-oriented or pedestrian-friendly. Developments designed to be safer and inclusive of pedestrians and promote walking rather than automobile use.

positive leverage. Borrowing funds and investing them for a higher return on equity.

pre-sales. Sales required by the bank (50 to 60%) before construction financing is approved.

pro forma. A multi-year cash-flow projection for a development project, calculating revenue, costs, and potential profit as the project evolves.

public realm. All the publicly accessible open space in cities, Inclusive of streets, parks, public parking, and other open space. The public realm also includes publicly accessible open space on private property and normally makes up 40 to 50% of cities.

redevelopment. Rebuilding of an urban residential, commercial, or other land use area that is in decline or in need of a new vision and policy direction.

residual land value. A real estate valuation metric used to help developers determine the appropriate land price to be paid. The equation used to calculate residual land value is the gross development value less the total project cost, including fees and developer profit.

return on investment (ROI). A performance measure (%) that evaluates the profitability of an investment. Simple return on cost or return on revenue calculations compare profit to cost or revenue on a static one-year basis. More complex cash flows over the period of development calculate a *net present value*

(NPV) or *internal rate of return (IRR)* and take into consideration various cash flows over time.

rezoning. A change of zoning required for a different land use and/ or density, which can raise the value of a property.

schematic design. Preliminary design for initial concept discussions, not as detailed as *design development*.

site form-makers. The important physical factors that shape the site and proposed built form. These physical factors can include vegetation, slope, watercourses, orientation to wind and sun, soils, and wildlife.

soft costs. Construction costs not directly related to materials, labour, or the building of the project (e.g., feasibility studies, land acquisition, permits and other fees).

suburban retrofit. The redesign and redevelopment of the outer edges of a municipality where there is lower housing density to allow higher housing density and multiple uses.

supply and demand. An economic model of price determination and fluctuation: given low supply, demand and prices rise; and given high supply, demand and prices fall.

tendering. The process in which a project invites qualified general contractors to submit bids to construct a project along with subcontractors.

term sheet. A non-binding agreement outlining the basic terms and conditions under which a real estate investment will be made. A term sheet is normally issued by a bank or lending institution.

units per acre (UPA) or per hectare (UPH). A density measurement for single to multiple housing units. Normally, 4 to 10 UPA relates to single-family housing; 11 to 20 UPA relates to townhomes or attached housing units; and 20 UPA or above relates to apartment dwellings.

working drawings. Precise scale drawings for construction that include structural, electrical, and mechanical specifications and other information relevant to the project.

NOTES

CHAPTER 1 | Overview of the Development Process

The epigraph is from Tony Robbins, "5 Keys to Rise in 2024," January 1, 2024, 1, https://www.linkedin.com/pulse/tony-robbins-5-keys-rise-2024-tony-robbins-pucwe.

1   Susan Goldenberg, *Men of Property: The Canadian Developers Who Are Buying America* (Toronto: Personal Library, 1981).

2   "Brookfield Consortium Acquires O&Y Properties and O&Y REIT," Lexpert, n.d., https://www.lexpert.ca/big-deals/brookfield-consortium-acquires-oy-properties-and-oy-reit/345764.

3   See Michael A. von Hausen, *New Pathways to Approvals: Developing Better Communities Together* (Victoria, BC: Tellwell, 2021), 241–254 and Appendix A, "Acquisition Comprehensive Checklist."

CHAPTER 2 | Influences and Future Thinking

The epigraph is from Bruce Katz, "How Cities Can Thrive in the New Industrial Era," *The New Localism* [newsletter], January 18, 2024, para. 1, https://www.thenewlocalism.com/newsletter/how-cities-can-thrive-in-the-new-industrial-era. See also Bruce Katz and Jeremy Nowak, *The New Localism: How Cities Can Thrive in the Age of Populism* (Washington, DC: Brookings Institution Press, 2017).

4   Harp Dhillon Group of RBC Dominion Securities, *HD Insights*, January 25, 2024, 1.

5   MLA Canada, *MLA Intel 2024 Report* (Vancouver, BC, January 2024), 7, https://mlacanada.com/newsfeed/mla-intel-2024-report-bcs-2024-real-estate-landscape.

6   William Ury, *Getting Past No: Negotiating in Difficult Situations*, rev. ed. (New York: Bantam Books, 1993), and *The Power of a Positive No: How to Say No and Still Get to Yes*, illus. ed. (New York: Bantam Books, 2007).

7   See Tom Durrie, *School and the End of Intelligence: The Erosion of Civilized Society* (Boston Bar, BC: Free School Press, 2022).

8   Malcolm Gladwell, *Outliers: The Story of Success*, reprint ed. (New York: Back Bay Books, 2011).

9   National Centers for Environmental Information, January and October 2024, https://www.ncei.noaa.gov.

10   Immigration, Refugees and Citizenship Canada, "Government of Canada Reduces Immigration," news release, October 24, 2024, https://www.canada.ca/en/immigration-refugees-citizenship/news/2024/10/government-of-canada-reduces-immigration.html.

11   Statistics Canada, "Canada's Population Estimates: Strong Population Growth in 2023," March 27, 2024, https://www150.statcan.gc.ca/n1/daily-quotidien/240327/dq240327c-eng.htm.

12   Kevin Hughes, "Increasing Productivity to Address Canada's Housing Crisis: Where Are the Gains?," CMHC (blog), March 7, 2024, https://www.cmhc-schl.gc.ca/blog/2024/increasing-productivity-address-canada-housing-crisis-where-gains.

13   David Gordon and Isaac Shirokoff, *Suburban Nation? Population Growth in Canadian Suburbs, 2006–2011*, Working Paper 1, Council for Canadian Urbanism, 2014. Professor Gordon of Queen's University authored with Remus Herteg the *Canadian Suburbs Atlas* in October 2023, updated with 2021 census data and completed while he was a visiting professor at the University of Toronto's School of Cities. Gordon worked with students at the University

of Toronto and Toronto Metropolitan University to develop this latest version of the research, which is unique in providing a detailed analysis of large and small cities across Canada. See https://schoolofcities.utoronto.ca/research/canadian-suburbs-atlas.

14 Metro Vancouver Regional Planning, *Costs of Providing Infrastructure and Services to Different Residential Densities*, September 2023, 5, https://metrovancouver.org/services/regional-planning/Documents/costs-of-providing-infrastructure-and-services-to-different-residential-densities.pdf.

15 Winston Szeto, "City of Kelowna Develops AI Tool to Speed Up Building Permit Applications," *CBC*, April 26, 2023, https://www.cbc.ca/news/canada/british-columbia/kelowna-ai-chatbot-building-permit-applications-1.6822450. For more information, contact City of Kelowna, Planning Development Services, https://www.kelowna.ca/city-hall/contact-us/general-inquiries-8.

CHAPTER 3 | The Place-Driven Idea

The epigraph is from Albert Einstein and first appeared in "What Life Means to Einstein: An Interview by George Sylvester Viereck," *The Saturday Evening Post*, October 26, 1929, 117, col. 1. See the Quote Investigator, https://quoteinvestigator.com/2013/01/01/einstein-imagination/.

16 Richard Florida, *Who's Your City? How the Creative Economy Is Making Where You Live the Most Important Decision of Your Life* (Toronto: Random House of Canada, 2008), 157.

17 Conversation with Andy Yan, director of the City Program at Simon Fraser University, Vancouver, BC, February 9, 2024.

18 See Legacy Farm Project, https://legacyfarmproject.ca/.

19 Michael A. von Hausen, *Public Realm: The New Makers Handbook* (Vancouver, BC: Tellwell, 2022).

20 "Estimates of Canada's Infrastructure Deficit Vary Widely," CanInfra, https://www.caninfra.ca/insights-6.

CHAPTER 4 | Market, Feasibility, and Finance

The first epigraph is from a CMHC news release, "Housing Starts Down 7% in 2023 from 2022," January 16, 2024, paras. 1–2, https://www.cmhc-schl.gc.ca/media-newsroom/news-releases/2024/housing-starts-down-2023-from-2022. The second epigraph is from a real estate company director of marketing, UDI School of Development event, Vancouver, BC, 2015.

21   Michael von Hausen, *Marketing Guidelines for the Nu-West Community* (Nu-West Development Corp., Calgary, AB, 1981).

22   Bank of Canada, "Bank of Canada Reduces Policy Rate by 50 Basis Points to 3¾%," news release, October 23, 2024, para. 8, https://www.bankofcanada.ca/2024/10/fad-press-release-2024-10-23/.

23   Loan to value ratio is the total loan compared to the appraised value of the property. If the loan is a relatively low percentage as compared to the value, it is a measurement that expresses lower risk of the investment. Be careful to review the appraised value of the property. It should reflect the comparative value of the property, considering the highest and best use, in the current marketplace.

CHAPTER 5 | Site Review and Testing

The epigraph is from Jordan B. Peterson, *12 Rules for Life: An Antidote to Chaos* (Toronto: Random House Canada, 2018), 98.

24   Don Vaughan, "Japanese Garden, Museum of Civilization, Gatineau, Quebec" (blog post, n.d.), para. 2, https://donvaughan.wordpress.com/landscape-architecture/parks-gardens/japanese-garden-museum-of-civilation/.

25   Michael A. von Hausen, *New Pathways to Approvals: Developing Better Communities Together* (Victoria, BC: Tellwell, 2021), Appendix A.

CHAPTER 6 | Partners and Elevation

The epigraph is from Stephen R. Covey, *Primary Greatness: The 12 Levers of Success* (New York: Simon & Schuster, 2015), 90.

26 Canada Lands Company, "Garrison Crossing, Chilliwack, British Columbia," 2024, https://www.clc-sic.ca/garrison-crossing.

CHAPTER 7 | Approvals

The first epigraph is from Roger Fisher and William Ury, *Getting to Yes: Negotiating Agreement Without Giving In*, 2nd ed. (New York: Penguin Books, 1991). The second epigraph is from Ken Blanchard, *Leading at the Higher Level: Blanchard on Leadership and Creating High Performing Organizations* (Old Bridge, NJ: Pearson Prentice Hall, 2007), 216.

27 British Columbia, Ministry of Housing, "Legislation Introduced to Streamline Delivery of Homes, Services, Infrastructure," news release, updated November 7, 2023, https://news.gov.bc.ca/releases/2023HOUS0063-001737; Kira Davidson, "New BC Housing Legislation Brings Changes to the Public Hearings Process," British Columbia Law Institute (blog), December 15, 2023, https://www.bcli.org/new-bc-housing-legislation-brings-changes-to-the-public-hearings-process/.

28 Michael A. von Hausen, *New Pathways to Approvals: Developing Better Communities Together* (Victoria, BC: Tellwell, 2021), 70–91.

29 Ibid., 114.

30 Fisher and Ury, *Getting to Yes*; Stephen R. Covey, *The Third Alternative: Solving Life's Most Difficult Problems* (New York: Simon & Schuster, 2011).

CHAPTER 8 | Construction

The epigraph is from the executive vice-president of a development company, Digging into the Dirt Behind Construction seminar, UDI School of Development, Vancouver, BC, February 8, 2024.

31   More information is available from the Government of British Columbia, "For Property Owners and Developers," updated August 2, 2024, https://www2.gov.bc.ca/gov/content/industry/natural-resource-use/archaeology/private-commercial-or-development-property.

CHAPTER 9 | Higher Returns

The first epigraph is from Winston Churchill, two-term prime minister of Great Britain (1940–45, 1951–55), responding to criticisms that he had changed political parties, https://www.brainyquote.com/quotes/winston_churchill_138235. The second epigraph is from Theodore Roosevelt, the twenty-sixth U.S. president, in his speech "The Strenuous Life" (1899), https://www.brainyquote.com/quotes/theodore_roosevelt_103499.

32   Stephen R. Covey, *The Seven Habits of Highly Successful People: Powerful Lessons in Personal Change* (New York: Penguin, 1993).

BIBLIOGRAPHY AND FURTHER READING

Anielski, Mark. *The Economics of Happiness: Building Genuine Wealth*. Gabriola Island, BC: New Society Publishers, 2007.

Auerbach, Herb, with Ira Nadel. *Placemakers: A Brief History of Real Estate Development*. Vancouver, BC: Figure 1 Publishing, 2016.

Beasley, Larry. *Vancouverism*. Vancouver, BC: UBC Press, 2019.

Berridge, Joe. *Perfect City: An Urban Fixer's Global Search for Magic in the Modern Metropolis*. Toronto: Sutherland House, 2019.

Blanchard, Ken. *Leading at a Higher Level: Blanchard on Leadership and Creating High Performing Organizations*. Old Bridge, NJ: Pearson Prentice Hall, 2007.

Carnegie, Dale. *How to Win Friends and Influence People*. Updated ed. New York: Simon & Schuster, 2022.

Caro, Robert A. *The Power Broker: Robert Moses and the Fall of New York*. New York: Random House, 1975.

Covey, Stephen R. *Primary Greatness: The 12 Levers of Success*. New York: Simon & Schuster, 2015.

———. *The Seven Habits of Highly Successful People: Powerful Lessons in Personal Change*. New York: Penguin, 1993.

———. *The Third Alternative: Solving Life's Most Difficult Problems*. New York: Simon & Schuster, 2011.

Fisher, Roger, and William Ury. *Getting to Yes: Negotiating Agreement Without Giving In.* 2nd ed. New York: Penguin Books, 1991.

Florida, Richard. *Who's Your City? How the Creative Economy Is Making Where You Live the Most Important Decision of Your Life.* Toronto: Random House of Canada, 2008.

Gladwell, Malcolm. *Blink: The Power of Thinking Without Thinking.* New York: Little, Brown, 2005.

———. *Outliers: The Story of Success.* Reprint ed. New York: Back Bay Books, 2011.

———. *Talking to Strangers: What We Should Know About the People We Don't Know.* New York: Little, Brown, 2019.

———. *The Tipping Point: How Little Things Make a Difference.* New York: Little, Brown, 2000.

Glaeser, Edward. *Triumph of the City: How Our Greatest Invention Makes Us Richer, Smarter, Greener, Healthier, and Happier.* New York: Penguin Books, 2011.

Goldenberg, Susan. *Men of Property: Canadian Developers Who Are Buying America.* Toronto: Personal Library, 1981.

Hansen, Mark Victor, and Robert G. Allen. *The One Minute Millionaire: The Enlightened Way to Wealth.* New York: Crown Business, 2002.

Harcourt, Mike, and Ken Cameron, with Sean Rossiter. *City Making in Paradise: Nine Decisions that Saved Vancouver's Livability.* Vancouver, BC: Douglas & McIntyre, 2007.

Hoggan, James, with Richard D. Littlemore. *Do the Right Thing: PR Tips for a Skeptical Public.* Herndon, VA: Capital Books, 2009.

Jacobs, Jane. *Cities and the Wealth of Nations: Principles of Economic Life.* New York: Random House, 1984.

———. *Dark Age Ahead.* New York: Random House, 2004.

———. *The Death and Life of Great American Cities.* New York: Random House, 1961.

———. *The Economy of Cities.* New York: Random House, 1969.

Lencioni, Patrick. *The Five Dysfunctions of a Team: A Leadership Fable*. San Francisco: Jossey-Bass, 2002.

Maxwell, John C. *The 21 Indispensable Qualities of a Leader: Becoming the Person Others Will Want to Follow*. Nashville: Thomas Nelson, 1999.

Peterson, Jordan B. *12 Rules for Life: An Antidote to Chaos*. Toronto: Random House Canada, 2018.

Punter, John. *The Vancouver Achievement: Urban Planning and Design*. Vancouver, BC: UBC Press, 2003.

Rybczynski, Witold. *Last Harvest: From Cornfield to New Town; Real Estate Development from George Washington to the Builders of the Twenty-first Century, and Why We Live in Houses Anyway*. Reprint ed. New York: Scribner, 2008.

Saul, John Ralston. *The Comeback: How Aboriginals Are Reclaiming Power and Influence*. Toronto: Viking, 2014.

Sipe, James W., and Don M. Frick. *Seven Pillars of Servant Leadership: Practicing the Wisdom of Leading by Serving*. New York: Paulist Press, 2009.

von Hausen, Michael A. *New Pathways to Approvals: Developing Better Communities Together*. Victoria, BC: Tellwell, 2021.

———. *Real Estate Economics in Urban Design: The Role of Civic Economics in Place-Making*. Vancouver, BC: Simon Fraser University, 2004.

Ury, William. *Getting Past No: Negotiating in Difficult Situations*. Rev. ed. New York: Bantam Books, 1993.

———. *The Power of a Positive No: How to Say No and Still Get to Yes*. Illus. ed. New York: Bantam Books, 2007.

Wickman, Gino. *Traction: Get a Grip on Your Business*. Dallas: BenBella, 2011.

ABOUT THE AUTHOR

Michael von Hausen developed and currently facilitates the FortisBC School of Development for the Urban Development Institute in Vancouver, B.C. He is also adjunct professor at Simon Fraser University, Vancouver Island University, and the University of the Fraser Valley. Michael is president of MVH Urban Planning and Design, a firm that supports developers, landowners, and municipalities in their quest for excellence in planning, design, strategies, and approvals. Michael has advised municipalities across Canada and has worked around the world. He is a Fellow of the Canadian Institute of Planners and a Fellow of the Canadian Society of Landscape Architects. Michael is a graduate of Harvard University with a master's degree in urban design and a specialty in real estate development economics.

His firm, in association with other consultants, has won numerous provincial, national, and international awards for outstanding planning, development, and design. These include two gold awards in 2023 from the Planning Institute of British Columbia, for the Garrison Crossing development in Chilliwack, B.C., and the Grand Forks Official Community Plan and Implementation. Michael has published numerous books and developed other publications. See the list that follows and for more details, go to mvhinc.com/books. Michael can be reached directly at vhausen@telus.net or through his website at mvhinc.com.

OTHER PUBLICATIONS
BY THE AUTHOR

The goal of these publications is to provide timely, affordable, and accessible information to advance climate resilient and smart urban design as well as sensitive and efficient land development planning. These publications are available at **mvhinc.com**, and the first four are available at **amazon.ca**.

Public Realm: The New Makers Handbook 201 pages, ISBN 978-0-2288726-8-9 (Tellwell, 2022)

New Pathways to Approvals: Developing Better Communities Together 274 pages, ISBN 978-0-2288-4196-8 (Tellwell, 2021)

Small Is Big: Making the Next Great Small and Mid-size Downtowns 204 pages, ISBN 978-1-928172-21-5 (VIU Press, 2018; Tellwell, 2019)

Dynamic Urban Design: A Handbook for Creating Sustainable Communities Worldwide 514 pages, ISBN 978-1-4759-4989 (iUniverse, 2013)

Urban Design and Planning Graphics Resource Book: Effective Visual Communications for Informed Decision-Making 170 pages (SFU, 2012)

Eco-Plan: Community Ecological Planning and Sustainable Design 158 pages, ISBN 978-0-86491-327-2 (SFU, 2011)

100 Timeless Urban Design Principles: A Handbook to Inspire Great Ideas 114 pages, ISBN 978-0-896491-289-3 (SFU, 2008)

Real Estate Economics in Urban Design: The Role of Civic Economics in Place-Making 25 pages (SFU, 2004)

Leading Edges: Alternative Development Standards in British Columbia Municipalities 30 pages, ISBN 0-9730290-0-5 (REFBC, 2002)

Michael A. von Hausen
FCIP, RPP, FCSLA, BCSLA, LEED®AP
President, MVH Urban Planning & Design Inc.
Telephone: 1-604-536-3990
Email: vhausen@telus.net
mvhinc.com